THE CREDIT BUILDING BLUEPRINT

7 Pillars to Excellent Credit

Chad Murray

Your Credit Coach

Copyright © 2019 by Chad Murray

All Rights Reserved. No part of this publication may be reproduced, stored in a retrieval system, or transmitted, in any form or by any means, electronic, mechanical, photocopying, recording, or otherwise, without the prior written permission of the publisher.

Printed In the United States of America

ISBN 978-1-7334196-0-4

The Credit Building Blueprint

Book Cover Designed By: Abir Hasan

Limit of Liability/Disclaimer of Warranty: While the publisher and author have used their best efforts in preparing this book, they make no representations or warranties with respect to the accuracy and completeness of the contents of this book and specifically disclaim any implied any implied warranties of merchantability or fitness for a particular purpose. No warranty may be created or extended by sales representatives or written sales materials. The advice and strategies contained herein may not be suitable for your situation. You should consult with a professional where appropriate. Neither the author or publisher shall be liable for any loss or any other commercial damages, including, but not limited to special, incidental, consequential, or other damages.

For general information on our other products and services, please contact us at www.yourcreditcoach.com

Within *The Credit Building Blueprint*, clients names have been changed to protect their privacy and identity.

First Printing, 2019

To my Princess Saniya
and my Prince
Noah. You give me life.

You inspire me more than you can imagine.
I love you more than you could ever know.

ACKNOWLEDGMENTS

Without the help of some very special people, this book would just be a collection of ideas in my head. I have to start by thanking Shakira Thompson. You helped me take this jumbled mess and organize it in a way that is bound to change lives. Your support has given me belief when I had doubts. I'm so grateful for the long hours you spent to mold this into a book I am proud of.

I want to thank Fred P. Banny for being my "Friendtor" and giving me the insights that kept me grounded on my mission to serve people.

Jean Alerte, you are truly an inspiration and role model in my life, highlighting what a great businessman and even better family man looks like. The first book you wrote opened the possibility for this book many years ago.

Betty Norlin, thank you for letting me know I had this book and much more in me, I thank you for seeing more in me than I saw in myself.

Carolyn Quinton, you have been a great connector and amazing cheerleader throughout this process and for that, I acknowledge and thank you.

Kelly Charles, there are few in life who's light shines so bright, it inspires rather than intimidates and you are one of those, thank you for lighting my path and helping to show me the way.

Louis James, you helped me to see this book as a vehicle to bring financial literacy to audiences beyond what I saw. I'm grateful for your vision.

Marcia Murray, since I was young you instilled the love of words in me. You have always pushed me to be the best man I could be and here I am today. I'm so grateful for everything that you are to me. Thank you Mommy.

To all of my clients, to your stories and scenarios that provided support for this book, I acknowledge your contribution and want you to know I thank and appreciate you.

To anyone who has helped and contributed to this work, I humbly acknowledge and thank you for your contribution.

If you know anything about me, you know immediately, my family means everything to me, without them, there is no me. My sisters and brother, my aunties and uncles. My cousins, my nieces, nephews, and godchildren. To my ancestors. I'm honored to acknowledge my family for all of your love, support, and for holding me down the way you do. There are not enough words to express how I feel about my family but in this instance, I'll settle for two, thank you.

PREFACE

In reflecting on my coaching clients for credit, real estate, and financial literacy programs for young people, I realized a book was a natural progression for me. I truly believe, the idea to write this book was born out of someone else's need for the information.

With a wide array of issues and challenges, the one thing that my clients have in common is they never learned about credit, money, or real estate in school. Neither did I. Most of us never really learn about these subjects until we mess up our credit, or are forced to find a home.

Inside the company I've built, **I AM** *your* Credit Coach, **I AM** *your* Real Estate Investor coach, and **I AM** *your* Youth Financial Literacy Coach. While I AM all of these things, I cannot be everywhere at the same time. But the books, the online courses, and the programs are extensions of me, allowing me to be wherever you are.

This book is part of my mission to coach and educate team players willing to set themselves up to win and win in the areas of finance.

I have a proven record of winning championships with my clients, the championships of life, that is.

Inside this book, you'll be able to gain an understanding of my coaching abilities with some of the strategies I share.

Every good coach has a playbook he studies and shares and every now and again he keeps some plays to himself. In order to find out what kind of coach I AM, you'll have to continue reading. If you do, I make a promise to you that you will obtain a championship within your finances.

If you're ready to win, say, "I AM READY COACH!"

INTRODUCTION

When I think of the title of this book, *The Credit Building Blueprint, The Seven Pillars to Excellent Credit*, I often think of the old cliché "From Pillar to Post." I've thought about it so much, I decided to look into its definition and origination. The term is over five hundred years old and means, in short, moving from one predicament to another and this is exactly what this book is all about.

This book seeks to, through inspiration and information, empower readers to build a new mindset around credit and finances. It's been said, a wise person learns from other people's success and mistakes. The "blueprints" or case studies I use throughout this book will highlight how people just like you were able to overcome their challenges. No matter how big or small, these winners followed a game plan with discipline and persistence to ultimately achieve their objectives.

I've had the great fortune to work with people to build their credit to buy houses, build businesses, and more. Over the last seventeen years, my work as a mortgage broker managing an office with more than one hundred loan officers, becoming a real estate investor, and a credit coach have allowed me to assist people who thought their credit goals were out of reach. To experience transformation starting from despair, to hope, to empowerment makes the accomplishments of my clients' credit achievements even more meaningful.

Every credit issue has an expiration date. With a commitment to go through the process, it is only a matter of time before credit scores increase and doors to opportunities open up. The key is commitment. Far too many people quit or revert back to bad habits before they are able to see the improvement consistency yields. Most of us never learn how to manage money, or build our credit, in school. This book is a practical, pragmatic guide showing you step-by-step how to get the credit you want.

With this book in your hands and Your Credit Coach on your side, your credit challenges have now met their match. Follow through with your desire to have great credit and all the things that come along with it.

Should you stick with me, by the last page, you will know exactly how to implement the Credit Building Blueprint.

TABLE OF CONTENTS

Chapter ONE

Laying the Foundation

"You don't have to be great to start but you have to start to be great."

~Zig Ziglar

Wherever you are with your credit today, chances are, you earned it. If you have a 750 credit score, congratulations, you earned it. Likewise, if you have a 450 credit score, you earned that too. The good thing is you have the power to change your life using the principles and resources in this book. With a plan of action, desire, and a S.M.A.R.T goal to pursue, you can achieve better credit.

The road to becoming better will be long for some and shorter for others. Regardless of where you are, the destination can be what you want it to be as long as you follow through. The thing everyone has in common is that you can't get to where you want to go unless you start.

A challenge stopping most people from the outset is the size of the goal or the challenge ahead. For example, when you think about buying a house, certainly, it can be intimidating.

You are choosing a place to build your future, raise a family, and commit to a mortgage that on its face is thirty years long. Not to mention, this commitment is required whether your job is going great, or if it's gone altogether. If you don't like your neighbors, you can't just pick up and take your house somewhere else. Interestingly enough, these are considerations, all before we start to talk about the process to get approved for a mortgage. The list of things one might fear in such a pivotal undertaking can get long.

While these concerns are valid, when you consider what home-ownership does for a family, it's more than worth it. Sure, it's rough to have neighbors you don't like, but it's equally worse, if not more, to have a landlord you don't like. If the feeling is mutual, a landlord can put you out with just a few months' notice.

The idea of paying a mortgage can be frightening, however, in most cases, it's better than paying rent you cannot build equity on. The advantages you gain from going for your big goals far outweigh the fear of stopping you from doing so. Worst case scenario, if it doesn't work out, there's always a landlord willing to rent their property.

The point here is to go for it! However, before you do, set your goals and create a plan.

The great Zig Ziglar said, "If you aim for nothing, you will hit it every time." It's very rare someone accidentally ends up with great credit. It's usually a function of responsible planning, timely bill payments, and not having an overdependence on credit. If you are at a point where you are looking to create a credit profile that is going to give you the financial empowerment to attain a big dream, like home ownership, it's important to set a goal and create a plan. Getting your credit report can give you a clear picture of how you have handled your financial responsibilities.

Your credit is your financial soul. Even if you haven't seen your credit report in a while, for the most part, you know it's bad if it's bad and you know it's good if it's good. Seeing the report will confirm your truth, in most cases, and show you the details you can address and build on, in every case.

The next step is setting your goals to attain the score you want, which will open the doors for the goal you want. Armed with this information, changes can be made, and progress can be measured.

Setting Your Goals

When it comes to credit, reaching your goals is a function of your financial alignment. To be a homeowner, you need to have a homeowner's profile. Your credit, savings, and income have to embody a person who is prepared for the responsibility of wealth building and wide-ranging expenses. There are many levels in the process of becoming a homeowner. Like someone who is driving cross-country, you know your destination may be California, but you can't get there unless you drive through many other states. Like these states, the steps within the home buying process have their own rules that govern how well you navigate through them. There's the credit building process, the down payment sourcing process, the house finding process, and so much more.

To find success with the overall goal, you must achieve a measure of success with each of these areas first. It is vital to break down each category and set a target to get you to your objective. One of the seven habits from Stephen Covey's, "*7 Habits of Highly Effective People*" is to "Start with the End in Mind." This means you should envision your end goal and work backwards to complete the required task. Each of these tasks are worthy goals that will yield a great result when they all come together. Breaking down the process may seem overwhelming but you only have to work on one at a time. Furthermore, there is an abundance of resources to help you as you go. You can have a realtor, a mortgage banker, a credit coach, and more to help you on your journey. With all these moving parts, choose one goal. The important thing to remember is if you start it, finish it. Countless people start saving money only to abandon the mission when there is a bit of a financial squeeze or worse, a sale of some sort.

My friend Lee's story captures the process of approaching goals one by one.

Lee's Story

When we started working on Lee's credit, his score was in the low 500s. While he made most of his payments on time he carried high balances on his credit cards and had numerous delinquencies on his student loans. We discussed him applying for down payment assistance and for the programs we looked into, he needed a credit score of 640.

He overcame his challenge by focusing on paying off one credit card at a time. By doing this, he was able to bring down the balances, one card at a time. He didn't have to worry about his "mountain of debt," he just had to focus on one item. Step by step, payment by payment, his debt gradually shrunk. Eventually, his balances owed went down and his credit score went up.

We simply focused on one thing at a time and executed with excellence. After that, we focused on other areas of his credit until his credit was in alignment with his home buying goals. He went on to buy a house in New York City. The point is, we all have issues blocking the path to a goal. When you set an intention and set a goal, the smallest victories matter. As the goals and successes get bigger and bigger, so do the results. You may start with something like tracking your spending for seven days. When you accomplish that, you will be more conscious of your spending habits, and more prepared to budget.

Lee's Blueprint

Here are the primary goals Lee pursued to buy his home:

1. Save 3.5% of the price of the property for a down payment.

Depending on your region, this number will be different, but the percentage will be the same. Budget your savings based on the amount of down payment you want to invest. The FHA Loan requires a 3.5% minimum down payment and conventional mortgages require 3%-5% minimum, but also require a higher credit score. Lee was able to successfully save this money but since he qualified for a down payment assistance program, he was able to keep most of what he saved. Now he has options to set other goals with his money.

2. Build His Credit

Starting with a thorough credit audit, we were able to see the areas of Lee's credit causing him the most difficulty and where the most points were hiding. His goals were to:

- Dispute the inaccurate negative items on his report. We challenged details like his old addresses and a mistake in how a credit card late payment was reported.
- Get into a student loan repayment plan.
- Establish new lines of credit to drive the score up. (*This was determined after we did a thorough assessment of his credit. This is not the right move for everybody*).

3. Enroll in a Down Payment Assistance Class

There are many programs across the country offering down payment assistance. Each class requires participation in an 8-hour class. At the conclusion of the class, participants are eligible for up to $30,000 in assistance based on income, family size, and where the property is located. Taking the time to find the right program for you can save you thousands of dollars and remove one of the biggest barriers for home ownership, the down payment!

4. Get Pre-Approved for a Mortgage

Most times, before a realtor would work with him, they'd ask for a "Pre-Approval" or "Pre-Qualification" letter. A Pre-Approval letter is provided by a lender to show you are "Pre-Approved" for a loan at a particular interest rate and loan amount based on your credit, income, and down payment. The lender reviewed Lee's credit, income documents for the last two years, and liquid assets to determine just how much home Lee should be shopping for.

A Pre-Qualification letter is based on a less rigorous process. The information about the borrower can be given verbally in some cases and does not hold as much weight as a Pre-Approval letter. At this point a buyer will be able to see how much "house they can afford."

5. Begin the Home Search

Finding the right home can happen at the first house you see. For most people, it takes up to a few months into their search to find the right home and to have the seller agree to sell at terms that work for both parties. Having a strategy on how often you look at houses and where you are looking is going to streamline your search. Your home search can begin with finding the right Realtor.

My friend's story is not unique. It was a matter of setting goals and following them. The reason so many people never set goals is because they see their big goals as too hard to reach. The saying, "The best way to eat an elephant is one bite at a time" is true, even though it's a weird saying. The big things that have transformed our lives and our world started with a goal and a plan to achieve it. Start with one focus within a big goal and it won't be as frightening. You don't just write a book, you start with one word that turns into a sentence, that sentence then turns into a paragraph, the paragraph is now a page, next thing you know, you have a chapter. You complete this process over and over until you have your finished work.

Like we broke down Lee's goals within the home-buying process, you can do the same thing and see a similar result. With the goal-setting process, you can choose goals such as increasing your credit score by fifty points. You could commit to saving ten percent of your income or even cut down on eating out. You can go big or small with your goals, but having a target to aim for will give you a reason to adjust your habits to get the results you desire.

This journey is a personal one, so don't worry about what matters to other people. Design the budget, finances, and the life you want. A great way to start is by choosing a S.M.A.R.T. goal. Lee started this process with fear and trepidation but he was brave. He reached his goal in becoming a homeowner. Now he's looking for his first investment property.

After you complete your next big goal, I wonder what you're going to go for next?

S.M.A.R.T. Goals

We all know we should set goals to get what you want, however, how do you set goals? Is it as simple as saying, "I want a million dollars" and watching it manifest? It's not. Like anything else, the better the system you have to accomplish anything, the more effective it will be. The method that sets the right foundation for you to actually accomplish your goals is the S.M.A.R.T. goal. This is how you can set the guidelines for success.

This particular method gives you a mechanism to choose and measure goals in a targeted way.

S.M.A.R.T. goals are:

Specific

Imagine you could get exactly what you want if you asked for it. What would you ask for? That's how specific your goals should be. If you made a vague request, then you'd get a vague response. A clearly defined goal would allow you and others to hold you accountable. When putting your goals down, try to answer the 5 "W" questions:

- What do I want to accomplish?
- Why is this goal important?
- Who is involved?
- Where is it located?
- Which resources or limits are involved?

To show you how this can work for you and your mission, let's use a sample goal.

Sample Goal: *Track My Spending for Seven Days*

Is it specific? Yes. We know when the goal starts and when it will be completed.

Measurable

Peter Drucker, the guru of management was right when he said, "What gets measured gets managed." With goals, it is important to be able to gauge the progress you are making. This way, you will know whether or not you are on track to accomplish what you set out to do. This is a great way to keep you motivated and energized as you meet your deadlines and stay focused on the target.

A measurable goal should address questions such as:

- How much?
- How many?
- How will I know when it is accomplished?

Sample Goal: *Track My Spending for Seven Days*

Is this measurable? Yes, indeed it is.

Each day, you will be able to see how much money you are spending and capture those small expenditures you may have overlooked in your budget. Using your bank statement and receipts, you will see the numbers tally up as the days go by.

Attainable

If you've never run a marathon, setting a goal to complete one without training is setting yourself up for a weekend with dim lights and ice cream to comfort you after you fail! Don't set yourself up to lose and be disappointed with yourself. Set a goal that will stretch you, but not break you. You want to reach a higher level, so go for it in a way that allows you to get there with dedication and hard work.

An attainable goal will usually answer questions such as:

- How can I accomplish this goal?
- How realistic is this goal?

Sample Goal: *Track My Spending for Seven Days*

Do you believe this is attainable? I hope you said yes, because, yes, it is.

This may be outside of what you do now, but this is a goal that can be done if you are focused and dedicated. Use tools when you can to make your goals "you-proof," if you can. Buying everything from a debit card and collecting receipts for everything else will make the process quite attainable.

Relevant

Does it really matter? If it doesn't, you shouldn't do it. Your goals have to make a difference in your life to be considered, otherwise, it's a waste of time.

A relevant goal can answer "yes" to these questions:

- Does this seem worthwhile?
- Is this the right time?
- Is it in alignment with my needs?
- Am I the right person to reach this goal?
- Is it applicable to a bigger goal?

Sample Goal: *Track My Spending for Seven Days*

Is this relevant? My dear friends, yes, I believe it is.

By tracking your spending for seven days, you'll be able to see some holes in your spending habits you may have glossed over in your budget. If you are yet to start budgeting, this is a great way to get in tune with what your expenditures really are.

Time-Bound

If you don't have a date, then you don't have a plan. Every goal needs a target date or else it just wanders aimlessly. This is what helps separate your daily tasks from your purpose. With a time limit set to your goal, you can move urgently and intentionally to make your goal come true.

A time-bound goal will usually answer these questions:

- When?
- What can I do today?
- What can I do this week?
- What can I do this month?

Sample Goal: *Track My Spending for Seven Days*

Is this goal time-bound? You've answered correctly, yes, it is.

This goal is to be continuous for seven days. Though it would be great to be a hawk about your spending daily, the timeline gives you an opportunity to check what you may not have before. It can also be the first step to a new habit that will make you the master of your money.

Listen to me, you can do this...so what is your goal? What is it going to take for you to get it? Declare what this next step in your life is today and take it. The difference between successful people and people who don't accomplish their goals, is action, or better yet, inaction. Goal getters are goal setters and go-getters. It's not enough to just think about what you want. It's not enough to plan for what you want. It doesn't come together until you act on what you want. With proper planning, goal-setting, and focused action, everything you desire to accomplish is within reach. It will take effort and it may take time but consistently grinding to meet the dates for your goals will open the door to what you want.

Credit is a challenge anyone can overcome with the right plan, patience, and action. Think about it. All negative items have to be removed from your credit report after seven years with the exception of bankruptcy, which is ten years. The problem most people face is that in those seven years, some of them give up, others never commit to changing the habits that damaged their credit, and others still see themselves as bad with credit and money. Bad credit is an event, not a person. The moment someone chooses something different, their credit is on the road to recovery. Are you ready to choose something better?

So let's go for it! Here is a goal setting worksheet. Take the time to set your goals for your credit, money, or whatever else you desire. Do a separate worksheet for each of your goals that matter.

S (Make it Specific) - What do you want to accomplish?

M (Make it Measurable) - How will you know when you have accomplished your goal

A (Make it Attainable) - How can the goal be accomplished?

R (Make it Relevant) - Is this goal worth working hard to accomplish? Explain

T (Make it Time-Bound) - By when will the goal be accomplished?

If you took the time out to make your goals and vision clear, congratulations! You have taken a significant step in getting to what matters to you most. Now that your goal is on paper, it is more real than it's ever been. If you haven't or won't, why not? Many of us have key elements in our lives that are the quicksand to our progress. What is holding back your progress? A lack of patience? Procrastination? Short attention span? Not enough training? Not good enough? Not esteemed enough? Not smart enough? Not strong enough? In most cases, that's what it boils down to. Some feeling of lack, inadequacy, or fear. If you've seen it in your mind, it's already yours. You don't have to be anything more than who you are to deserve it.

For instance, let's take a look at Chris.

Chris' Story

A man who bounced from foster home to foster home as a child was working at a job for $8,000 a year. One day, he saw a man pull up in a Ferrari, wearing the nicest suit he had ever seen. He went up to him and asked, "What do you do?" The man said he was a stockbroker. From that moment, this man made up his mind that he was going to be a stockbroker. There was just one problem. He didn't know anything about stocks. There was also the fact that he had no connections, no money, no free time, and he was older than everyone who was getting ready to start their career as a stockbroker. He had nothing working for him. The only thing he had in abundance was problems and belief.

Chris' Blueprint

His first goal wasn't to be a multi-million dollar stockbroker. It was to build a relationship with the stockbroker he met. Then he set his attention on getting into the training program that the stockbroker told him about. Next, was to excel in the training program and get selected for one of the few positions being offered. Then his goal was to make twice as many sales calls as anyone else in the company. At that point, his goal was not to make enough money to buy a house and a car, and start his own firm, then sell it, then be a millionaire coach who travels around the country telling people that they can do it too! That's just what happened as he reached one goal and then the next. Sounds like a great story, doesn't it? The only thing I left out is that on the road to accomplishing his goals, this man had a few challenges.

As if his task wasn't already an uphill battle, he was only making $8,000 a year at a job that demanded all of his time. He was trying to provide for his girlfriend and his young son, but it just wasn't enough. He finally got the opportunity to get into the training program. He spent months building the skills to become a successful stockbroker and took home very little pay for the training but he was only months away from making more money than he could dream of. He ended the program at the top of his class. It was time for him to get his big break when the broker who introduced him to the company got fired and he got fired with him.

Back to square one. Would you give up? Would you say, "This just wasn't for me?" Chris didn't. He got accepted into another training program. This one, however, paid nothing at all! With no money and a young son to feed, he made the choice to give his son food and gambled on shelter. He moved from homeless shelter to homeless shelter. He and his son even slept in a public bathroom one night when the shelter was full. Imagine sleeping in a public bathroom at night then working in a financial services office the next day. He amassed over $1,200 in parking tickets to get to his training meeting and was eventually arrested and put in jail for ten days for chasing this dream. He suffered, and suffered, and suffered some more because he knew that whatever pain, shame, and seemingly insurmountable odds he had to face, this was what he was going to do, period. That's the power of making a decision.

This man is Chris Gardner. You may be familiar with him and his story from the movie, *The Pursuit of Happyness*. It's an adaptation of his life's struggles and ultimate success. He's an inspiration to many. There are many financially successful people out there but they made a movie about his life because he exhibited something rare in the world: He exhibited the ability to go through challenges and never stopped until he achieved his goals.

You will face obstacles on your journey to your goal. You may feel like an obstacle is getting the better of you. That's okay. People expect the journey to success to be a straight line, but in reality, it will take you places you never thought you could go and places you never thought you could come back from. What Chris Gardner's story shows is the power of seeing your goals through. It may not work when you plan on it, or when you want it to, but if you resolve to make this dream happen or else, there are only two options: success or death. At least you won't feel like a failure if you don't get your dream in time. What have you been working on that matters to you? Is it building your credit, starting a budget, or writing your business plan?

If it matters to you, put it down on paper and work on moving it from a someday dream to an on-this-day goal.

Your Blueprint:

- Keep in mind, you don't have to be great to start, but you have to start to be great.
- Anything you want starts with the first step.
- Like Lee, you may be a long way from your goal when you start, but with consistent work, you can reach your goals and more.
- Start by declaring your goal.
- Use the S.M.A.R.T Goal system to make your goal a real target.
- Once you've set your goal, get it, no matter the cost, like Chris Gardner.

Chapter TWO

Give Yourself Credit

"Don't let what you cannot do interfere with what you can do."

~John Wooden

Some say "Cash is King." Is it really? Jobs don't check your "cash" to see if they should hire you or not. The cash most of us can save won't be enough to buy a house without a loan. The impact of credit goes far and wide. Everything from finances, to employment, to car insurance is affected by your credit. As powerful and important as it is, most people never take formal classes to learn about the details of credit and how they can use it to better their lives. Unfortunately, most people never really get serious about credit until they either mess it up or get denied for it. Without the proper education on credit, consumers have gotten themselves into significant debt, collections, and bankruptcy. I'd venture to say if cash is king, then credit is the kingdom.

Credit is a topic often approached with fear because while it is known that bad credit can ruin areas of your life, few know how to build credit effectively and fewer still know how to maximize its use. The good thing is, the credit system is forgiving. While creditors will hound you relentlessly, the credit reporting agencies allow you to redeem your credit woes over time. If you've experienced financial hardships that led you to poor credit, I have great news for you, you won't be condemned for life. With the right strategies and commitment to better financial habits, credit scores can increase, even if you've had a foreclosure or other credit crises in the past. The key thing to know is if you are willing to do what it takes, you can get the credit you want. The goal of this book is to give you information you can apply to experience transformation. As my friend Jason Lee says:

Information + Application = Transformation

What Is Credit?

Credit is a measure of your financial integrity. It is a system that has evolved over millennia from before 1800 BC when The Code of Hammurabi put limits on how much interest could be charged on grain and silver.

In modern times, credit reporting agencies buy, sell, and maintain personal information about your payment history, employment history, addresses, and more. These multinational corporations measure the likelihood of you defaulting on your bills by using algorithms that consider everything including how you've paid your debt in the past, how much debt you carry, and how long you've had credit.

There are five primary factors used in determining a (**FICO**) score, which is a numeric grade given to your credit based on a model developed by the Fair Isaac Corporation. The credit score you earn over time determines your ability to attain credit. It affects the interest rates you are charged, the amount of credit you are given, how much money you'd be required to put down on a house, and so much more.

How credit is experienced has changed over time, but ultimately it comes down to how reliable you are at giving back what you borrowed.

You can see this play out in grade school playgrounds. One child will bring in their prized toy to school and is the star of the playground because everyone wants that toy and now, here it is. Usually, one child is able to convince another to hold the toy for a while. Every now and then, when school or recess is over, the borrower breaks the toy or does not return the toy to the lender. Kids cry, parents are called, and cool toys are banned from schools. What do the rest of the children think about the borrower? Would they lend him their toy after seeing what their classmate went through? Definitely not! There's no numeric grade the borrower in this case gets, however, his unwillingness or inability to return what he borrowed will leave a lasting impact on the rest of the students.

This is how credit works.

Whether on the playground or your application for a house, how you've borrowed in the past is going to affect your ability to borrow today.

Most of us desire to be high credit character people. What's the difference between those who actually have great credit and those who don't?

The majority of my credit clients have faced some form of financial hardship driven by a lack of a game plan on how to pay their bills. Fewer people understand when, how, and why to use credit. Others are so scared of credit they don't use any at all. At their detriment, they are missing out on the possibility to leverage credit, to grow wealth through equity in a property, or by funding to expand their business.

Don't let that be you.

Lack of education can be a reason to move slow but not a reason to stop moving forward. Take this process slowly, but keep taking one step at a time. As you learn and implement positive credit principles, the results will show on your credit report. Balances will decrease and credit scores will increase over time. You'll find the process of building credit can be one of the most empowering experiences you can have.

Why Credit Matters?

Good credit is the gift that keeps on giving. When you have good credit, you'll be offered more credit than you'll ever need. If you have bad credit, you won't be able to get the credit you want. It impacts so many areas of life that without credit you can be without a job, house, car, and opportunity. Money can't buy happiness but poor credit can bring you misery. Here are just a few areas of life that your credit is impacting your potential:

Real Estate

Real estate is the number one vehicle for wealth in the country. It gives people the opportunity to live in an investment or getting paid for having people live in their investment. The price of real estate requires most Americans to get loans to purchase the homes they live in and the property they use as an income generator. People with poor credit are unable to get funding for a home without a large down payment. For these people, poor credit can cost them a significant portion of their wealth and the option to leverage credit to grow wealth.

To purchase a home, banks can require a credit score as low as 580. While mortgage requirements change, what is constant is better credit gives you access to better interest rates and more money. If someone purchased a property for $100,000, and in 10 years, the property's value increased by $50,000 to $150,000, they would have earned $50,000 of wealth. Compare that to someone who pays $1,000 for rent for the same 10-year timeframe. They would have spent $120,000 and would not have gained $1 of wealth through equity. That's a difference of $170,000. Unfortunately, millions of Americans are making the decision to pay rent and miss out on wealth through equity because they don't have the credit to make home ownership possible.

Mortgage credit requirements may change to make home ownership easier to achieve or more difficult, but based on the numbers, it's worth it for your financial future to build credit to have the option. So many people don't even consider the possibility of home ownership because of credit. What if I told you the credit requirements for a mortgage are more lenient than the requirements to get a low interest rate auto loan?

Auto Loans

Buying a car is less of a luxury than it is a necessity these days. With busy lives including work, school, childcare, and groceries, cars make our lives work. That's why people are willing to pay high interest and put themselves into bad debt to keep up with their lives.

According to Manheim Used Car Market Report for 2017, 1.8 million vehicles were projected to be repossessed. The high interest rates consumers are paying on car loans are not only costing them up to hundreds of dollars a month but also, in 1.8 million cases last year alone, it's costing them their credit.

A repossession is one of the harshest penalties credit consumers can face. A good credit score can help consumers pay lower down payments and lower interest rates. It will also help to avoid late payments or repossession because lower down payments and lower interest rates lead to lower payments and more affordable financing. While automobile financing can give you the freedom of the open road, expensive financing can be a burden that can get you stuck in financial quicksand. With good credit, you drive within your budget instead of having high-interest rates driving you crazy.

Personal Loans

Whitney M. Young, the civil rights hero, once said, “It’s better to be prepared for an opportunity and not have one than to have an opportunity and not be prepared.”

When life gives you unexpected opportunities or expenses, having access to credit can make all the difference in the world. If your air conditioning goes out in the summer or your hot water heater goes out in the winter, a personal loan can save the day.

Personal loans are loans given by banks They are unsecured and credit driven loans. People use personal loans to pay for weddings, funerals, debt consolidation, and more. It’s important to be very prudent with your credit decisions like this, yet having the option is better than having bad credit, and fewer options.

Furthermore, in the event of an unexpected expense, having the required credit score can help you weather a storm when you do not have the money on hand. With poor credit, expect to be denied for one of these loans. Like other loans, the amount of credit you will get access to and the interest rate will be based on how high the credit score is. This proves not being prepared with good credit could leave you out in the cold if your credit can’t support you when the unexpected happens.

Business Credit

Whether big or small, credit is used to take businesses to the next level. Business owners use credit to get inventory, expand, and to float expenses until invoices are paid. A business can build credit independently of the business owner's personal credit, yet, with strong business credit and strong personal credit, a company's purchasing power can grow exponentially. Businesses are either growing or dying. Stagnation means a company won't be able to invest in marketing to keep up with competitors. They won't be able to invest in technology to make their operations more efficient or hire more associates in an effort to grow.

When businesses begin to contract, credit can be the solution to inject capital in order to spur growth. Business owners with poor credit are often forced to consider high-risk loans with high-interest rates and daily payments. As a result, they get stuck in a cycle of treading water just to be able to pay the bills and keep the doors open.

For instance, the difference in payments for a Merchant Cash Advance compared to a Small Business Administration (**SBA**) Loan can be 20-30% a month. A Merchant Cash Advance is a loan given to a business based on its monthly deposits with less focus on the business owner's credit. These loans charge interest and collect a payment from a business every business day over the course of a short loan term. A Merchant Cash Advance can cost a company 20-35% of each credit card transaction the business generates until the full amount of the loan is repaid. How do you think that impacts their bottom line? Many businesses who utilize the services of Merchant Cash Advances find themselves in a constant and desperate search for money. Whereas a business loan would give them relief and the ability to reinvest. Short term cash advances often keep them in business with just enough to stay afloat but not enough to grow.

Standard business loans on the other hand give business owners the ability to invest and grow, without the strain of giving up a percentage of their daily revenue. The Small Business Administration, or **(SBA)** is a government agency that provides support and resources to small businesses. They make loans through banks, credit unions, and other partner lending institutions. SBA Loans are based on the prime rate and can be as low as 4.5%. The loan repayment times are from 10-25 years so a business can adequately plan for the future. SBA Loans typically require a business to be established for three years or more and for the business owner to have a 675 FICO score or more.

The difference in the loans available for poor credit business owners and strong credit business owners can be the difference between thriving and surviving, success and failure. Business owners who don't have the financial discipline to maintain good credit often lack the discipline to handle a company's finances in a responsible way. No matter how good the product is, it won't be able to be produced at an affordable cost, marketed to the buyers who need it, or give the company the profit it needs because of poor credit. However, with good credit, all those things are possible because the cost of money impacts the business in every way.

Business credit can open companies up to significant growth and credit is a driving factor in how a business is funded. Low-interest rates make it possible for high profits while high-interest rates respectively, mean less profit. This could be a determining factor in the success or failure of your business. With both strong personal and business credit, your company will have more options than those with neither.

Getting Your Credit Report

With advances in technology, most often, when traveling to unknown destinations, what do we now do? Through our smartphones, we input the address from our current location and leave the rest to the mapping software housed within the Global Positioning System (**GPS**).

When you are setting your GPS to get to your destination, the first thing you have to know is where you are now. If your goal is to get better credit, knowing what's on your credit is your starting point, your current location. Obtaining your credit score is the first step to improving your credit. Having the knowledge of what's on your credit can empower you to be able to do something about it and move in the right direction, ultimately leading you to your final destination.

Kimberly's Story

One of my clients referred a friend to me, her name was Kimberly. In meeting her, I discovered Kimberly had been in a bad relationship with credit for the last ten years. During that time, she hadn't applied for any new credit because her credit history was so bad she thought, "I don't want to waste my time."

She received a letter stating her rent was set to increase by an additional $200. Interestingly enough, her rent was already as high as some people's mortgages.

Receiving the rent increase notification triggered Kimberly to make a decision towards repairing her credit and becoming a homeowner.

After telling me over and over her credit was so bad and her credit profile was going to be one of the worst I'd ever seen, I was expecting the worst. However, when she finally built up the courage to get a copy of her credit report, she couldn't believe what she saw. Her credit score was around 670 and the report was clean.

Like many Americans, yes, she'd experienced financial hardships during the downturn of the economy in the early 2000s. Credit card bills were unpaid for all of those years and other than a high-interest car loan she had been paying on for years, there was no positive credit. Given that, how could her credit score be so high and what happened to all of the negative items that kept her credit low for so long?

First of all, bad credit is not a life sentence. Negative items are required to be removed from credit after seven years. Bankruptcy can stay on credit for up to ten years. Credit is a "what have you done for me lately" deal. Once Kimberly took the time to get her credit report, she was able to face her new reality. The credit storm had passed and the one thing left on her credit report was a car payment she'd been paying on time. Her credit score was way better than she thought and she would have never known it without her landlord raising her rent. Sometimes bad news can turn into an unexpected blessing.

Think about how many people believe they can't buy a house because their credit is bad, but have not looked at their credit report in years. The psychological impact of negative credit can cost you more than the financial impact of credit in some cases. Not only are people, like my client, missing out on opportunities, but also they're living with the shame of old issues that matter more in their minds than in reality. Time and again, I experience people who will swear their credit is horrible just for the credit report to be a pleasant surprise. Checking credit reports quarterly allows you to check for any inaccuracies and be clear about where your credit is so you know how to govern yourself accordingly.

Kimberly's Blueprint:

- Life can be easier with better credit. Don't accept poor credit as your way of life. When Kimberly finally faced her credit fears, her score wasn't nearly as bad as she thought.
- By getting a copy of her credit report, Kimberly was able to see where she was in order to choose where she wanted to be.
- Bad credit has an expiration date. Just because you ***HAD*** bad credit does not mean ***YOU*** are bad credit.
- Check your credit report quarterly to check your progress and to verify that only what belongs on your credit is being reported.

According to the Federal Trade Commission (**FTC**), 20% of credit reports contain some form of error that can negatively impact your credit. Your credit is the gateway to opportunities ranging from home ownership, business financing, and even employment. Unless you have a copy of your credit report, you can't be certain your credit is in the best possible condition to get you what you desire.

The Fair and Accurate Credit Transactions Act of 2003 (**FACT Act**) allows all consumers to get a free copy of their credit report every twelve months. Annualcreditreport.com is the only government endorsed resource for your free credit report. This website allows you to see all of the details on your credit report. Each report contains credit information and personal information about you that can support you in getting to your goals or be in the way of what you want. Annualcreditreport.com is limited because it doesn't give you your credit score for free. You have to pay an additional fee for the credit scores. As a result of the FACT Act, numerous companies offer a free or inexpensive credit report with a membership to credit monitoring. That means you will get the credit report for free or close to it, but will have to pay to maintain the service. These services allow you to get regular updates on your credit report, credit education, and other resources that can support you in achieving better credit. Here are a few places you can get your credit report and what they offer:

The Big Three:

Each of The Big Three credit bureaus, Transunion, Equifax, and Experian offer credit monitoring for a fee. You need to monitor each of your credit scores and credit reports but you do not need an account with each bureau. If you did, you would have to purchase an account from each of the three bureaus and monitor each one separately. That's just too much time and money. Of the three, Experian offers a tri-merged bureau report for a one-time fee of $39.00, while Equifax offers a tri-bureau report annually for a fee. For monthly credit bureau monitoring, each of these falls short of the best options. These are some other options that could better serve your needs:

FREE Credit Monitoring Services:

There are several free credit monitoring services available online. The focus here will be to highlight some of the more popular options. Many credit card companies offer free credit monitoring. Therefore, as a credit card customer, you may be entitled to this free service. While they mostly don't give you access to your credit report, they will give you monthly credit score updates, usually with one of the three credit bureaus.

Credit Karma:

This online service is absolutely free. You can get your Transunion and Equifax credit reports along with their respective scores. The great thing is like other credit sites, they offer useful tips on credit and give text and email alerts. Fortunately, unlike other sites, they never require a credit card.

On the downside, the scores are rarely accurate. The scores you see on this site are considered VantageScores, a consumer scoring model, developed by the big three credit bureaus, designed to compete with the FICO scoring model.

There are cases in which they give you a higher or lower score than what other sites would give you. In addition, neither your Experian credit report or score are available through this service.

Each bureau can report different items and scores on credit. Therefore, not having all three bureaus will leave you with only a part of your credit picture. Credit Karma is great to start with, but not good enough to bank on for your next big credit mission.

Creditsesame.com:

Credit Sesame offers their credit monitoring through Transunion. With them you get a free credit report and monitoring each month. They also give you $50,000 in identity theft insurance and fraud resolution assistance for free. The additional resources make Credit Sesame great value. The drawback is you only get one credit report a month. You will only get one- third of your overall credit picture and you have to wait for the most up to-date version of your credit report.

As far as a free service goes, however, this is good for informational purposes. With credit having such a significant impact in your life, good won't be good enough if you are working towards a particular objective. If you are casually keeping tabs of your credit and like the idea of their identity theft insurance and fraud resolution assistance, this is definitely a viable option.

MyFICO:

In my opinion, MyFICO, is the best site you can get for accuracy. They use twenty-eight different versions of your credit score which are used by mortgage lenders, auto dealers, and credit card companies. When you sign up, you will get instant access to your tri-bureau credit reports and scores. The service comes with email and text alerts for changes on your account such as an inquiry, a new collection account, an address, late payment, newly opened account, change in your balance, and so much more. However, the shortcoming to this service is it only updates the credit report and score every quarter.

At the time of writing this book, MyFICO Ultimate 3B Credit Monitoring subscription is $29.95 a month or $329 for a yearly subscription. You can cancel the service at any time.

PrivacyGuard:

PrivacyGuard provides credit monitoring for all three credit bureaus along with your credit scores from each. Their daily credit monitoring sends you alerts by text, email, or your phone anytime your credit report information changes. PrivacyGuard's service comes with a trial for just $1.00 for the first 14 days. After that, you'll be charged the monthly subscription fee based on the plan you choose.

PrivacyGuard offers basic ID Protection for $9.99 per month. ID Protection scans for signs of identity theft by monitoring both the public and Dark Web, public records, and more. A strong feature of their program is, they offer up to one million dollars in ID theft insurance as a part of this subscription. Credit Protection for $19.99 per month includes your three-bureau credit reports and scores, along with daily credit monitoring. The credit score simulator allows you to get a sense of how certain changes to your credit will impact your score. The Total Protection plan is $24.99 per month and includes all the features of the Credit Protection and ID Protection Plans.

More information on Privacy Guard can be found on their site, https://www.privacyguard.com.

Identity IQ:

Identity IQ has been in business for more than twenty years. Their credit monitoring service provides identity theft protection for your credit reports from all three of the major credit bureaus. Credit scores are included in each of the subscriptions you can choose from. They offer Value, Total, and Premier Plans for an individual and/or a family.

Like PrivacyGuard, their plans include one million dollars of identity theft insurance, which is a high level of protection in the event your identity is compromised. They also have a case manager to work with you if your identity is stolen. You can utilize their mobile application to access your membership information, alerts to your personal information on the Dark Web, monthly credit score, and three-bureau credit monitoring.

Plans range from $8.99 to $24.99 for individuals and $14.99 to $34.99 for family protection. Some subscriptions include a $1.00 trial. If you decide not to keep your subscription, make sure you cancel before the trial ends to avoid charges.

If Identity IQ appeals to you, more information can be found on their site, http://bit.ly/idiq365.

Each and every day, a new credit monitoring website and app hits the market. Therefore, be careful with your information and only use credible choices.

All in all, take the time to get a copy of your credit report and you'll be on the right path towards taking control over your credit. Knowledge is power and with the knowledge of what's on your credit report, you'll have the power to intentionally choose which direction to move in towards a final destination of better credit.

In seeing the entire scope of your credit history, you can 'map' out a plan, such as challenging inaccurate items and having them, while at the same time surveying the areas that require work and attention.

Five Credit Factors

Like any good relationship, credit takes time to build, and yes, at this point, you are now in a relationship with your credit. You can start to establish a high credit score quickly, but the aim is to maintain it. Using good habits, tools, and techniques, you can create a credit profile that will help you to buy real estate, get money to fund your business, and so much more. With credit playing a role in the job you get, the amount you pay for insurance, and the college you get to go to, credit is a life skill that has a far-reaching influence on your life. Things like employment, race, or income, don't play a role in your FICO Score, so your credit score is all about what you do, and not who you are. This section will help you to accomplish your credit score goals.

The habit needed to help you to have control over your credit rather than it having control over you, is budgeting.

According to Dave Ramsey, "Budgeting allows you to tell your money where to go instead of wondering where it went."

When you are intentional about how you use your income, you'll be able to keep your debt at a point of serving your goals. Many Americans live with credit treating it like an untamed animal. Once it gets away from you, you'll spend valuable time trying to catch it before it does damage. This skill will support you in every area of your finances. In particular with credit, it's the difference between maintaining and building a strong score and hoping you don't end up with a bad score. Credit is a tool, but for many, it becomes a lifestyle. Without a game plan, the most trivial expenses are added to credit, costing you money and debt in the long run. Adopt the habit of budgeting and your credit will thank you.

If you already have established credit, the easiest way to improve your score is by paying down the balances on your lines of credit. The other factors that determine your credit score don't offer you as much control as you have with controlling how much you owe. If you keep a high balance one month and pay the balance down the next month, you can drastically improve your score in no time.

In comparison to payment history, if you are over thirty days late one time, it will take time for your subsequent timely payments to undo the damage of the initial late payment.

In addition, keeping your credit balances to less than 30% of what you owe will optimize your credit score as well.

The most obvious and most important thing you can do to build your credit is to always make your payments on time. Don't borrow above what you absolutely know you can pay back. Using credit sparingly with an end goal in mind will support you in being strategic about your credit. Go into using credit with a game plan from the start and you'll be prepared to pay off what you owe on time or sooner. Setting up systems can help you to make your payments without having to think of it. If you can set up automatic payments, as long as there's money in your account, you'll be able to make payments and not have to worry about writing a check, making a call, or anything. The payment is made and your FICO score is happy, rewarding you with a nice score.

Spending within your means is the key principle that will make everything else work. If you spend more than you make, your budget will never work, and automatic payments will eventually be automatically overdrawn. If you feel like you're on quicksand with your money, I guarantee there are some places where you can cut spending, change habits, and make your budget work. It will take a focus on choosing to go for what you want most, over what you want now. It may not seem like it's within your control, but just like the driver who took a wrong turn, you have the power to get back on track. My challenge to you is to cut one thing from your monthly expenses to make a difference in your entire financial picture. If you need some suggestions, look at what you're spending to eat out. What about clothes, socializing, or online shopping? It may not be easy, but it will be worth it.

Here is a breakdown of how each of the five factors impacts your FICO Score:

- Payment History: 35%
- Utilization Rate: 30%
- Length of Credit: 15%
- Credit Mix: 10%
- New Credit: 10%

We will now go through and explore how the five factors come together to compute your credit scores. Every financial move you make has an impact on your credit, and with this series, you'll be able to find points to add to your credit report with purpose and direction. Transunion, Equifax, and Experian can give you three different scores because different credit companies report to some and not others. We can't figure your score down to the exact point, but understanding the principles we are about to go into will give you the power to use five different paths to increase your score.

Payment History

The first part of the equation is payment history. Your payment history accounts for 35% of your credit score and essentially, this is the part that you have the most control of every month. Ultimately, this comes down to how well you make your payments. If you make your payments on time, it's going to report positively to the credit bureaus. It does not report negatively until you're over 30 days late, so essentially, every 30-day mark you do not make a payment is going to be a new negative connotation on your credit report.

The way it reports is, if you're late 30 days, it's going to report 30 days late. If you're late 60 days, the reporting shows it, then it will report 90 and 120 days as well. Once you get past 120 days, you're going to be looking closer to becoming a charge off, which is the next level of negative reporting to your credit. The goal is to be able to make your payment on time every time. By doing so, 35% of the job is done and you'll be well on your way to having good credit.

There are three things you can do to make sure your payments are made on time as much as possible and they are as follows:

1. Always put it on your calendar to make your payments. Whether you have it so all of your payments are made on a particular day or all of the payments are scattered throughout the month, always put it on your calendar. Once it's on your calendar, you have extra notice to make sure you can be intentional about making those payments on time. Using your calendar to help organize your payments is a proactive step that can go a long way.

2. Always have your payments scheduled and arranged based on what works for you. If you have one payment due on the 1st, another payment due on the 15th, and another payment due on the 17th, you can schedule to have your due dates changed to suit your income schedule. You have the power to call up each and every one of your creditors and have them set your payment for when you want it to be due. Ultimately, by doing this, you could have all of your payments scheduled for one day, or as many days as you need to make it work for your income schedule. If you need, you could schedule it around when you get paid but the goal is for you to be intentional about when you make your payment. If you take the power over when you make the payment, your debt will have to work around your schedule and not the other way around.
3. The most important thing you can do is to have all of your payments automated. By having your payments automated, you don't have to think about it. You get to set it and forget it! Well, not quite forget it. You have to regularly check your bank accounts and statements to make sure the correct amounts are being taken out at the right time. Also, with all the bank fraud going on, you always want to know what's happening with your bank accounts. The great thing about automated payments is, as soon as the day comes when your payment is due, it'll be done, and you'll have a positive note on your credit report. Whether you decide to schedule all of your payments to be due on one day, or if you choose to keep the due dates as they are, you can maintain and build great credit automatically. Once you've done this, you'll be in a position where 35% of the credit equation is in your favor every month.

Utilization Rate

Your utilization rate is the ratio between how much credit you have available as opposed to how much credit you've used. Fundamentally, the more credit you have used, the higher your risk factor is. There's an inverse relationship that occurs here, the higher the risk you are, the lower your credit score becomes. On the other hand, the more credit you have available, and the less of it you use, the credit score increases.

The maximum percentage of credit used should be 30%. If you have a $1,000 credit line, the most you want to use is $300. To get the most out of credit utilization, keep credit balances at 10% or lower. This can be the difference between good credit and excellent credit. While a borrower can get financing for houses and cars with a 30% utilization rate, credit scores and borrowing capacity will increase with lower credit usage.

Your utilization rate is responsible for 30% of your credit score. You'll always want to be mindful to keep this particular factor at the forefront of everything you do credit-wise. With utilization rates, there are a few things you can do to make sure it is in the best standing possible. The first thing you can do is, the obvious, either reduce the percentage to 30% or if it's already there, keep it there. Maintaining the utilization rate will report positively each month.

Being debt free is the best possible outcome for your finances. In terms of your credit score, having a small balance reflects more positively than no balance. Therefore, carrying a zero balance can have a negative impact on your score. With that in mind, it is up to you to be strategic with how you approach your credit. Carrying a small balance can help your credit score prior to making a major purchase such as a house or a car. Once you get to your initial goal, the best goal is to eliminate your debt by paying off your balances.

From there, the next thing you can do is schedule to have your payments due three days before the payment reporting date. This is a small detail that can lead to great results. By doing this, if your payment is due on the first, you could arrange where the creditors don't report it to the credit bureaus until the fourth of the month. In doing this, you're putting yourself in a position where you've made your payment and when it's reported to the credit bureaus, it's reporting at the lowest balance for the month. Depending on how much you owe and how much you pay down, you could see a significant improvement to your credit score within a month, or more. This strategy is simple and will really make a difference. Once you set this up, you'll experience the residual effects on an ongoing basis.

The last thing you can do to optimize your utilization rate is to request credit limit increases. Every six to nine months, you can be eligible for your creditors to increase the limit on the credit available to you. If you have a $1,000 credit card with a balance of $500 and you increase the limit to $3,000, it will drastically decrease your utilization rate, which would increase the positive scoring for this credit line. Credit limit increases will only be given to consumers who have good credit. If you are currently delinquent on other lines of credit or maxed out on credit cards, creditors most likely will not increase your credit limit. Practice good credit habits and this option will be available to you to great effect.

Length of Credit

Length of credit is a key element of credit scoring strengthened by time. This is a factor that doesn't leave room for many options to improve upon. Credit, like a lot of other things in life, is based on a relationship. The longer the relationship with credit, the better it is for you. If you're able to maintain a positive credit history over time, you will see your credit score improve gradually, with time.

For example, if somebody has been able to make all of their payments on time for an entire year, compared to somebody who has been able to make all of their payments on time for ten years, who do you think is going to have a better credit score? With all other factors the same, the person who has established credit over a longer length of time will have better credit. A longer history of on-time payments will allow this borrower to qualify for higher credit limits, lower interest rates, and a wider range of financing options.

What you can do to ensure the length of credit works in your favor is not to close cards with established credit history. Even if you've had late payments, even if it's been in bad shape in the past, you want to do all you can to bring the card current and keep it open. Once you are able to build positive, consistent payment history, you'll benefit from the line of credit being opened for an extended period of time. If you close a troublesome card, you're going to take away what had been a burden but you are also going to take away the length of credit that would be a blessing for your credit.

Credit Mix

Your credit mix is pretty much a measurement of how well you've diversified your credit usage. Ultimately, are you only using credit cards, or are you using credit cards, an auto loan, a mortgage, and an installment loan? What this shows is how responsible you are in being able to manage different kinds of debt.

Credit cards are the easiest type of credit to get and unfortunately, many people develop a credit card dependency. Using varied forms of credit shows a high level of responsibility. It indicates you are obtaining credit purposefully, not just because you can get it. If you only have credit cards, your credit profile will be limited. If you are able to get credit cards, an auto loan, and a mortgage, the diversity in credit will allow you to have a higher ceiling for how high your credit can go. Credit mix isn't the biggest piece of the pie, but if you use it the right way, it could be the difference between your credit being good or excellent.

Understanding these five factors will help you take advantage of credit score points that are currently not working for you. By implementing the strategies laid out here, you will benefit your credit score and have access to more and better credit.

Your Blueprint:

- Know what you need credit for so you know what you're building towards.
- Use your credit report like you use a GPS. Know where you are starting in order to get to where you're going.
- Automate your credit payments to make good credit automatic.
- Keep your credit balances below 30% of your credit limits to have good credit.
- Keep your balances around 10% to have great credit.
- Do not close established credit lines. The longer they are open, the more they improve your credit score.
- Remember, it's just credit. You have accomplished many more important things in your life. Be sure to give yourself credit because you are doing great.

Chapter THREE

Counting the Costs

"A budget is telling your money where to go instead of wondering where it went."

~ Dave Ramsey

NBA great, Shaquille O'Neal, was mic'd up at an NBA All-Star game when he made a joke about fellow Hall of Famer, Tim Duncan. After Tim Duncan scored a basket with a very technically sound move, Shaq gave him the nickname, "The Big Fundamental." It was hilarious and it stuck with him for the rest of his career! All the players on the bench, his teammates, were rolling over laughing as were the commentators, as well as myself at home watching.

As funny as it was, Tim Duncan's mastery of the fundamentals made him unstoppable. He's arguably the best who ever played his position and has championships and Most Valuable Player accolades to prove it.

That's what budgeting is, the "Big Fundamental" of finance. It's not flashy or even fun, but it will allow you to plan out your financial future like nothing else. It is the basis of good credit and is one of the best financial habits you can develop. Many people who have had credit challenges in their past end up experiencing credit issues again because the source of their credit woes are poor financial habits. To create a lasting change in credit and financial health, there are a few simple yet powerful tools that can make all the difference. To begin with, a foundational rule in personal finance is to spend less than you make. The problem is some people never stop spending until their money is gone. This is often a result of a lack of discipline but also an absence of a personal financial plan.

"But don't begin until you count the cost. For who would begin construction of a building without first calculating the cost to see if there is enough money to finish it?"

Luke 14:28 (**NLT**)

In reading this book, you are at least, in some way, interested in how to build excellent credit, am I right? Well, whether you believe in the Bible or not, the aforementioned words from the scriptures ask a very important question, who builds without first counting?

As we begin to count, a budget is a detailed outline of all your income and expenses for a given period. Setting goals and clearly defining your actions to meet these goals is the key to budgeting. Budgeting helps you to prioritize your spending in the order of importance. By doing this, you are now able to manage your money to eliminate wasteful spending habits, thus, channeling your income in the right direction to achieve your financial standards. According to a survey done by Forbes

Magazine, only 37% of Americans have enough savings to pay for a $500 or $1,000 emergency. The Pew Charitable Trusts also report one in three American families have no savings at all. Budgeting decreases surprises and stress levels. Knowing exactly where you are spending your money allows you to gain financial clarity.

Budgeting can help you to realize your wealth with a few simple approaches. Like any other great achievement, discipline is required. Like most things, I'm sure you've heard the saying, "There's more than one way to skin a cat" Well, budgeting is no different. Based on your preference, there are a number of strategies available to choose from, given your particular style and lifestyle.

Take stock of your financial situation. How much do you own and how much do you owe? Many of us feel as if we know what our financial status is, but in reality, most people are assuming and not assured of their financial standing. By now, have you identified your financial goals? If so, what is the timeline for you to accomplish them and how far along are you? Just the idea of having to look in the mirror and accepting the reality of one's financial position is enough to cause stress and panic for some. When you consider the social security income our grandparents were able to live off of is less than guaranteed for our generation, we are being irresponsible with our lives to not face these facts head-on. However, a budget can prepare us for this reality.

A great place to start is by getting your bank statements, tax returns, and credit reports together. With these key documents, the numbers will reveal themselves. If you thought you were on your way, confirmation lies in these documents. If not, you get the opportunity to recalibrate your current habits and structure a plan of support designed to assist with your intentions.

The 50/30/20 Rule

This powerful and popular tool sets you on track to build your budget by giving a guideline for your needs, wants, and savings. According to this method championed by Senator Elizabeth Warren, 50% of your income should be assigned to needs, 30% to wants, and 20% to savings. This is a very conservative model asking you to save a lot of your income. The long-term gains can be immeasurable.

Needs:

Your needs include rent or mortgage payments, car payments, groceries, insurance, health care, minimum debt payment, and utilities. Some things like your coffee habit or a new car may feel like needs but they are not essential to make life work. Needs are expenses vital for survival. If you are looking at your needs and saying, “There’s no way that all of my needs fit into 50% of my income,” you may be living above your means in one or more of these areas. When you are starting out, don’t expect everything to be a perfect fit. The first step is to set the 50/30/20 ratio as a marker. From there, start to cut costs in the areas you can control.

Our needs, wants, and savings will change over time. Maybe an emergency caused you to go into debt at some point in your life. Maybe it was youthful indifference or just not knowing any better. Nevertheless, do what you can do today and make a positive change. Target bills in the "need" section of your budget and work to eliminate them while resisting the temptation to add to your expenses in the wants category. In time, 50% of your income required for this system will become more of a reality.

Wants:

Your wants can be summed up into all of those things that make life more comfortable and enjoyable. Wants can account for the difference between an economy car, which can be a need versus a luxury vehicle, clearly a want. It also includes the difference between dinner and going out to eat. All of your entertainment, such as cable television and going to the movies are accounted for here in the "wants" area.

Clothes are a necessity; if you don't believe me, go to work without them and see what happens. Those designer shoes, fancy handbags, and name brand clothes do however cross the line from a need to a want.

Comfort and necessity are not the same. While we all want to live our best lives with the best the world has to offer at our fingertips, our desires should come after taking care of the basics.

I once had a client, Nicole, who would have a steak for dinner coupled with an octopus appetizer every Friday after a long week at work. It was her treat to herself for surviving the work week and celebration for not losing it with the crazy people at her job.

When I asked her if she would be willing to cut out this expense to pay down her debt, she said, "I work hard and feel like I deserve to be able to treat myself to dinner on Friday." It is very important to reward yourself for the work you do in the office and home, but at what cost? My client eventually realized her $65 meal was costing her more than just $3,380/year. It was also costing her interest on the credit card debt she incurred every Friday evening.

Nicole was on track to spend $3,380 in one year for her fancy weekly dinner date. You may think she was wasteful–but what are you wasting money on? Is it shoes, vacations, or drinks at the bar? Don't get me wrong, you can't buy peace of mind, so when you find a routine to unwind and relax, embrace it. On the other hand, be intentional about doing it in a way suitable for the bigger picture. With Nicole, she decided she loved her Friday date nights with herself but she also chose to be more responsible with her finances. She found a restaurant that provided her with a nice dining experience for less than half the price. The trick is to look at ways that you can do what you love to do in a more financially responsible way.

Savings/Debt

According to Gobankrate.com, 57% of Americans have less than $1,000 in savings. The 20% recommended for savings in this ratio, is one that is a huge stretch for many. If you have a retirement plan, that will be included in the percentage of your total savings. To make this strategy most effective, maximizing your pre-tax savings plan will make a portion of your savings automated. This is a gradual process, so be sure to eliminate high-interest debt before you maximize savings. Credit cards can charge you double-digit interest rates. Saving money at 8% annually while you pay 18% monthly can have you saving at a deficit.

Remember, there is no expectation for you to be at the 50/30/20 budgeting percentages when you start. Like a runner whose time for running around the track will get better and better with practice, you will get closer and closer to ideal budgeting ratios as you commit to eliminating debt, spending intentionally, and saving. The sooner you strive to live by the 50/30/20 rule, the easier it will be. The reason saving is challenging for so many Americans is, we are entrenched in our bad spending habits that have been developed and strengthened over time. If you are just starting out in your financial life, having this strategy as the basis of your finances will allow you to achieve financial freedom exponentially faster than someone who has to eliminate significant debt and break bad spending habits.

The 20% of your budget is also allocated for debt. While the priority is to make all your monthly payments on time, use this portion of your budget to eliminate debt. Depending on which strategy works best for you, you can pay off your debt targeting the smallest debt first or the highest-interest debt. The idea is to be consistent and committed to this process. Anyone can be on point with this budget when things are going great. Those who are able to keep the progress going, regardless of external circumstances, are the ones who achieve success with their budgets and many other areas of life.

As you break down your income based on this method of budgeting, don't be discouraged if you are not in alignment with this strategy now. For many, the idea of having a plan for one's money is a new concept. Be patient and forgive yourself if this doesn't become your lifestyle right away. With this system, the 20% you are saving on every paycheck will have a huge compounding effect that will pay a big part in how your financial future plays out.

The Envelope Method

One of the more popular and old-school styles of budgeting is the Envelope Method. My grandmother used to always have different envelopes with cash for different purposes. She had one envelope for gas, one for groceries, and others I never thought to ask about. One envelope was money from her tenants. I don't know what she used it for, but I always thought it was cool to see her counting all that money. If only my grandmother would have told me what she was doing, she could've saved me so much of the money I blew in my twenties. She was practicing an age-old method geared towards budgeting cash and managing money like a pro. One of the key reasons the Envelope Method works so well is because it's a tangible way to manage your money.

With this strategy, you mark envelopes for your monthly expenses. The envelopes can be used to separate your money into categories like your groceries, entertainment, clothing, and even charitable giving. This is a great way to manage variable and leisure expenses. With the technology available to us today, more people budget with online tools and apps, but this way makes each dollar matter much more because you can see it and feel it before it leaves your care. This is one of the best ways to give each dollar an assignment.

To start the Envelope Budgeting Method, write out your budget for all of your income and expenses. Then take one of the categories you are budgeting for and grab an envelope. If you have budgeted $400 for groceries for the month, take $400 out of your bank from your paycheck. If it would take you two or more pay periods to meet your grocery limit, that's fine. What makes this system work? It works because the $400/month put into this envelope is strictly used for groceries and groceries alone. Whenever you are buying groceries, you can only use the money from the "***Grocery***" envelope. Once the envelope is empty, the money assigned for groceries for the month is done. There are no loans from other envelopes or "IOUs."

In order for this system to work you have to hold yourself accountable for the commitment you made. By committing to this routine, you are agreeing to give yourself a spending plan that'll create discipline in spending and financial planning. If you overspend and can't buy something you needed to buy, simply, go without it. That way, the next time you go shopping, you'll be conscious of what an impulsive buy is costing you. This will limit impulse shopping and encourage more thorough budgeting. Maybe you didn't set aside enough money for groceries and too much money for entertainment. The first step is to put it all down on paper. Next, practice shopping based on your Envelope System. You may need to adjust your entertainment budget in favor of more groceries. If you make an adjustment to your envelopes, make them with your end-game in mind. Don't adjust to make yourself more comfortable. Instead adjust to keep yourself on track. Similarly to braces, I hear they're not comfortable and don't particularly look great all the time; however, when teeth are trained to be in perfect alignment, the smile to come is beautiful. Embrace the discomfort of this new financial habit. Once your money is in alignment with your purpose, the sacrifices made will be worth it.

What many people have found is the Envelope Budgeting Method allows them to make that trip to the store more organized and intentional. You are more likely to stick to your shopping list because you have a plan. Items that aren't necessary are less likely to find their way into the shopping cart because you've decided where you want that money to go already.

The biggest challenge to finding success with the Envelope Budgeting Method is technology. We have transitioned into an electronic society. Shopping, banking, and even budgeting are now done online. Having to go to the bank or the ATM makes this a cumbersome process. With our busy lives, adding another errand can make this a less appealing option for financial planning. For this same reason, it can hold more value. When you have to consider the work required in getting cash, it can be harder to let it go, compared to swiping a card. Having the physical, cold hard cash in hand is a tangible screening mechanism that judges the worth of each item purchased. So, while the drive and inconvenience of getting the cash is an obstacle, this method can be an obstacle to prevent unnecessary widgets and trinkets coming home with you.

Getting good at the Envelope Method can take some time. It can be a bit confusing at times as well. What should you do if you go to the store and buy $40 worth of food, $20 worth of clothing, and $30 in school supplies? That would be three different envelopes at one store. It may be a bit more complicated, but sticking with the system will keep you in line with your plans. Give yourself time to be able to adjust to transactions like this, which will surely occur especially around back-to-school season. Search online for a "Virtual" Envelope, which could be a good middle ground for you.

Zero-Based Budget

What you measure, you can manage. With the Zero-Based Budget, you are tracking every dollar and every expense. The purpose here is to calculate every dollar going to expenses but also being intentional about every dollar left over. Is your extra money going to debt, savings, or someplace else? Either way, this method audits your monthly flow down to the penny. This way, budgeters are able to plan how long it takes to pay off debt, how long before you can get the down payment for that house, and any other financial goals you may have. This is a more tedious method of budgeting. Be that as it may, imagine if your GPS dropped you off in the general area you are looking to go to. You wouldn't be very happy, now would you? No, you wouldn't and your budget isn't happy without precision. Precision does matter and the Zero-Based Budget ensures it.

This method of money management makes certain, if you bring in $4,000 a month, $4,000 a month goes where it is supposed to. Like any other personal finance tool, you're going to take care of your housing expenses, car, and other needs and then proceed to pay for your debts, wants, and savings. Unlike the Envelope Method where there is a possibility for a surplus, the Zero Based Budget isn't a success until every dollar is accurately applied to its specific task. You will have to hold yourself accountable and diligently track your money. This can feel like a job that restricts you, but in reality, it's giving you the freedom to work towards any goal you can shoot for.

Celebrate the Good Times

Getting your envelopes right for the month is a big deal! When you start out, you may experience growing pains. When you get to the point where you have money left in your envelope, you've won and winning is cause for a celebration. Therefore, celebrate your success. If you can do this in one area of your finances, think about what is possible when you are consistent in managing all of your money for the month. We're talking about a shift with significant implications of long-term financial growth and peace. Here's where you can give yourself a pat on the back, acknowledging your hard work and praising your dedication. However, make sure your celebration doesn't undermine the work you've already done. With what money is left over, use towards your savings or towards paying off debt and your financial dreams will manifest and find you faster.

Jodi-Ann's Story and Blueprint

I did a credit workshop for a group of about fifty people in New York City. The audience was very open and interactive. People shared their issues with credit and money and I gave as much information as I could to help. It was fantastic.

When I was done, I spoke with a number of the guests, beyond my normal greetings. One particular attendee waited patiently to greet me. I recalled seeing her during the presentation and remembered she hadn't said a word in the workshop but I could tell she wasn't leaving until she spoke to me.

With the room finally clearing out, Jodi-Ann made a beeline for me. She was both tense and pensive. She was facing a dilemma, she told me.

Her parents were moving out of the country and wanted to sell the house she lived in her whole life. Her parents offered her first right of refusal with time to build her credit and ultimately purchase the home, but time was running out.

She believed she hadn't done enough to secure the home and was afraid she'd missed her chance to take ownership of her childhood home.

In explaining the details of what her parents requirements were and the challenges standing in her way; I believed there was still a chance.

I felt there was still a chance to acquire the home, but I knew Jodi-Ann would have to be laser focused.

"Are you ready?" I asked.

With a slight pinch of trepidation, Jodi-Ann replied, "Yes, I'm ready."

The challenge Jodi-Ann faced was, even though she made good money, she didn't budget. As money came in, it quickly went out and Jodi-Ann had no idea where it was going.

She told me she was totally committed to doing whatever it took to buy her house and that's what I wanted to hear, because in most cases, that's all it takes.

Jodi-Ann didn't have any major habits, like shopping, nor was she a weekend warrior of any sort. She simply wasn't able to tell where all her hard-earned money was going. As we got started working to beat the clock, the first thing we did was to have her go through her last three months of bank statements. The last month told us what she spent, but the last three months told us what she consistently spent money on.

We discovered early on eating out in New York City where she worked was almost as bad as having a shopping habit. It was costing her almost $40 a day, five days a week, which equaled an $800 monthly expense.

From there, we also found a major surprise. She had been giving the maximum contribution to her retirement account at work. With the money she'd been making on paper, it didn't feel like she was seeing anywhere close to it, and this was the biggest reason why. This, of course, was a huge blessing–wherein it initially felt like a curse because it wasn't being properly accounted for. Best of all, if she was facing a real financial deficit, she could always restructure the amount she contributed monthly, freeing up available resources.

The next thing we did was we created a monthly budget. With the last three months of records, Jodi-Ann was able to be really clear about her monthly expenses and her monthly targets. She now knew one of the biggest things working against her and knowing she was doing great from a retirement standpoint gave her more confidence. While she wasn't able to spend money from her retirement account, it could be used for a down payment and to show money in reserves to acquire a mortgage. Things were looking a lot brighter already.

The first month of budgeting was a nightmare for Jodi-Ann. She enjoyed cooking, so bringing food in for lunch was one way she was going to curb her spending. The problem was she found every way in the world to leave her food at home. One day, she left it on the counter, another day in the Uber. It was like the restaurants of NYC were conspiring against her to keep her coming. Month after month, she trained herself to spend less eating out and to only spend what she had budgeted for. In only four months, she was able to have her proposed budget and her actual budget be within 10% of each other.

She was focused and ready!

Jodi-Ann got excited about how the control of her money was in her hands...which resulted in more of it in her pocket. Given her commitment to budgeting, she was able to pay extra money on her credit cards and in four months, her credit score increased by over 110 points. Jodi-Ann followed her blueprint closely in order to become a homeowner and now it was closer than ever before.

Jodi-Ann built a new habit that was yielding phenomenal results and getting ready to change her life. She already possessed everything she needed, but once she started tracking her money and spending, it all became clear to her. The work she had to do with her credit was manageable because she had a plan. She could now start to plan for the down payment, closing costs, an appraisal, and an inspection.

During that time, Jodie-Ann didn't get a pay raise or change that much in her life. What did change was the fact that she got focused.

Major deadlines could be exactly what you need to motivate you to get the job done in your life. Don't let that be the case. Set a target using your budget and stick with it. Jodie stuck with it. As a result, she was able to qualify for a mortgage and close on her house. She made a commitment and the commitment paid her back with the title of homeowner.

Your Blueprint:

- Create a budget to tell your money where to go rather than wonder where it went.
- Understand the difference between your needs and wants.
- Select the budgeting tools and techniques that work best for you.
- Find a more cost effective way to do what you love to do.
- When you meet your budgeting and saving goals, celebrate, then make new goals to attain.

Chapter FOUR

Focus - Follow One Course Until Successful

"Focus on where you want to go, not on where you were or where you are."

~Anthony Robbins

The late Pastor Myles Munroe is credited with saying, "The cemetery is the richest place in the world. In the cemetery there are books that were never published, inventions never built, and masterpieces never painted."

"People die with their gifts still in them," he proclaimed.

For those who've died without emptying out their greatness and fulfilling their dreams, I often wonder, what kept them from realizing their dreams.

They, like many of us when faced with the enormity of a big project, get overwhelmed. Questions like, "Am I good enough?" or "Can I do this?" swirl around in the mind of doubt, thereby poisoning their passions, leaving them to live beneath their divinity.

Some of the greatest achievements have been made by conspicuous characters who rose to meet a need for society or through a need of their own self-expression. The difference between names that history remembers and most others is the determination to see the journey through to completion, especially when it gets hard.

Colonel Sanders is a household name. Everyone has seen him or a character playing him in a Kentucky Fried Chicken (**KFC**) commercial. It feels like he and KFC have always been one of the most notable names in fast food, but this was no overnight success story.

Colonel Harland David Sanders was a serial entrepreneur. He did everything from selling tires to founding a ferry boat company. He tried and failed, then tried some more and failed more with some successes along the way. His road to notoriety did not start until he became a professional chef at the age of 40. He created his "Secret Recipe" at the age of 50. When he was 62 he franchised his Kentucky Fried Chicken "Secret Recipe" for the first time. He spent the next seven years traveling the country cooking his world class chicken recipe and attracting new franchisees. His company exploded and there were more than 600 locations internationally when he sold the business. He sold his company for $2 million at the age of 73 and was given a salary to stay with the company as a brand ambassador.

As a jack of all trades, Harland David Sanders was marginally effective with his efforts. It wasn't until he honed in on one target, then he became the "Colonel," who's chicken recipe is sold all over the world. Mediocrity takes no time, but greatness does not have a time limit to it. It requires dedicated work UNTIL the ultimate success is found. The cornerstone to massive success is FOCUS. **Follow One Course Until Success.**

Let's talk about it. What do you think keeps people from pursuing their passions? Is it the size of the task? Is it money, is it time, is it lack of support from family and friends?

Whether it's writing a book, building that invention, or painting a masterpiece, there comes a point when you have to reach a level you have never experienced before. Being great is a choice we all get to make. Some of us have moments, while others make greatness a lifestyle.

Take for example the sculpture of David. imagine if Michelangelo was sculpting The David, one of the most famous sculptures in the world, by working on one eye and then jumped to his left leg, then his right shoulder. It wouldn't be the genius work of art that it is. The detail and proportion of a nearly 17-foot man chiseled out of marble could only be done if each finger, nose, and foot was worked on with complete focus and continuity. In contrast, our culture celebrates the idea of multitasking, which leaves many people conditioned to work on many things and complete very little. The feeling of being busy is more important than the results they produce.

Michelangelo's David took three years of his life to complete. Today, people are always looking for a "microwave solution" for everything. Perfection takes time, along with dedication and focus.

I've had clients who have accumulated over $100,000 worth of debt, and then wanting credit repair to making it all magically disappear. As I told them, there is no shortcut to real progress. Debt has become the killer of dreams, the suppressor of hope, and the mountain responsible for blocking the views of better days.

Within my business, I do see where people are trying to do the best they can to conquer this beast, but their techniques and lack of strategies cause them to feel hopeless. As our discussion continues with dreams and FOCUS, we will shift the conversation to include debt and its elimination.

Jeanette's Story

For instance, a former client, Jeanette, a single mother of four, with one child plagued with persistent medical issues, was drowning in over $80,000 worth of debt. While she was a responsible woman, she was faced with the choice of taking on more debt or watching her child suffer and possibly die. For any parent like Jeanette, the answer was an easy, "Then debt it is." Respectively, when she finally came to a point where the health issues subsided for her son, she was intent on paying off her debt and restoring her credit.

She took on the approach of paying extra on every bill she had, even if it was just an extra $10. After almost a year of doing this, she noticed her mountain wasn't shrinking, and for some creditors, the amount she owed was increasing!

She began to lose hope.

If Michelangelo would've taken the chisel here and a little chisel there approach, he would have taken forever to create a disproportionate monster and not a masterpiece. That's what Jeanette was doing. When I started working with her, the first thing I expressed to her was, "You're not alone."

As a matter of fact the accumulation of debt has become a way of life for Americans.

Consumer debt for 2018 reached $3.945 trillion dollars, a new record for debt, with each year beating out the previous year's record. Debt allows us to leverage our limited financial resources to borrow money. When you consider that everything from a mortgage to a car loan to student loans are debt, it's safe to say most of us are "in debt." Conversely, debt is not all bad. If you build your credit, you are able to take advantage of an array of financing options. Strong credit individuals are able to borrow money at a low cost. This gives them the opportunity to buy real estate or even invest in their education at a reasonable amount of interest. The challenge we face is without the required understanding of debt, we have created a culture of overleveraged spenders with high amounts of money owed and very little saved. There are a number of crisis level debt problems coming for those who aren't financially prepared.

Jeanette had a serious problem, but with FOCUS, she had all the solutions she needed in front of her. I confirmed her strategy of paying more was the right idea. I explained when you pay more than the minimum payment to any bill, every extra dollar goes towards the principal balance. She had the right idea with the wrong execution. She was sprinkling her money around instead of blizzarding one creditor at a time.

If you've ever lived in New York in the winter you know that snow can be powerful. During a blizzard, there is a high concentration of snow in one area. If that same amount of snow was sprinkled around over many states, it would look beautiful coming down and harmless as it crunches slightly under your feet.

That's the stuff tourists love to see.

Yet it is a slightly different story when it's coming down like clouds falling to the earth. In it, you can feel like you're trapped in a snow globe. You can't drive, you can hardly walk, and you can't find enough clothes to keep you warm.

That's the difference between spreading small amounts of money to all of your creditors rather than focusing as much money as possible on one debt. I introduced Jeanette to two strategies that would help her to see the fruits of her labor. The Debt Snowball and the Debt Avalanche methods are two of the best proven ways to attack debt. Now she was armed with strategies coupled with focus and consistency, preparing the way for her mountain of debt to melt away in a predictable amount of time.

Debt Snowball

The debt snowball method is one of the most effective and efficient ways to pay off debt. It allows consumers to build momentum while seeing debt get decreased and eventually eliminated by consistently sending payments, and extra money to your bills in a strategic way. Paying Interest is one of the biggest killers of wealth, so with the debt snowball method, it aims to eliminate interest payments by paying off the principal balance faster. It works best after you've completed a monthly household budget. At that point, you'll be able to predictably see how much money you will be able to put towards your debt snowball every single month and how soon you can eliminate debt.

The key to this method is paying off your debt one item at a time. You are going to start by paying off the smallest item first. This way, it allows you to see tangible results along with small victories that build upon each other, invoking momentum, until you're debt-free.

You begin by itemizing all of your debts starting with the creditor, the balances owed, and the minimum payment. After you've listed them from smallest to largest, set all of your monthly payments to the minimum amount. Once you've completed your monthly budget, you'll be able to see how much money you have left over to pay towards your debt. Send every additional dollar at your disposal towards the smallest debt owed.

For example, if you have three credit cards: one with a $1,000 balance, one with a $5,000 balance, and one with $7,000 balance, you're going to be sending extra payments to the one with the $1,000 balance and if you end up with an additional $200 every single month and the minimum payment is $50, you'll be able to predict you could pay this debt off in four months. That way, you can see your debt has an expiration date and you can work as quickly as possible to get there.

The beauty of the debt snowball method is I've had clients start out with enormous mountains of debt, but after paying off that first debt, they got a huge psychological boost. They get a boost of momentum and energy propelling them into paying off the second one as soon as possible and then the third, and so on and so forth. The real key to this success is instead of it being an overwhelming process, all of the attention, all of your energy, and all of your extra money is just focused on one bill at a time. You can handle one bill, can't you?

Once you've listed out all of the debt you have to pay off, start making extra payments on the smallest balance. After four months according to the example above, the entire balance would be eliminated. With the first debt paid off, you've successfully eliminated the $1,000 balance. Congratulations!

Moving on, you're going to take the minimum payment from the first debt and roll it over to the second smallest bill. The second smallest bill, using our example, has a $5,000 balance with a minimum payment of $100. Now, the new payment you're going to send out, includes the previous minimum payment of $50 plus the $100 minimum payment, totaling $150 for the monthly bill payment instead of $100. It's the same amount of money going toward your bills, but now it isn't being sprinkled around, it's laser focused towards eliminating debt one payment at a time. Keep all other minimum payments scheduled accordingly until it's show time for them.

Now, this isn't going to show up on credit reports, it's not going to show up on the bill, but when you actually make your payment and you discipline yourself to at least make that $150 payment right away, you'll be sending more money towards the principal balance, paying off that $5,000 balance significantly faster than you would have organically. In addition to the additional $50 from the previous minimum payment, whatever additional money is left over after you've budgeted, is also going to be applied towards the principal balance.

Therefore, using the example of the $200 we previously discussed that was left over in the budget, is now added to the $150 payment, making it now a $350 monthly payment going directly towards the elimination of the $5000 debt. With this larger sum of money, you will be able to eliminate $5,000 of debt at a faster rate than before.

To calculate the time it would take to pay it off, divide $5,000 by the available $350 allocated. This equation easily illustrates, it would take a little more than fourteen months to pay off this bill. Keep in mind, as you go, you will see the balance decrease and your credit score increase. This process can be an exhilarating experience!

Guess what? In less than a year and a half, you've now eliminated two of your major debts. Congratulations! At this point, you turn all of your attention to the next debt. Your next target is the $7,000 balance with a minimum payment of let's say, $150.

If we add the $50 from the first paid off item, $100 from the second paid off item, the extra money from the budget for a faster payoff, $200, your monthly payment would be $500, instead of the minimum $150. Are you starting to see how momentum is built through this process? In this scenario, by spending $500 a month to eliminate a $7,000 debt, it would only take 14 months to do so. Based on this example, you can see how you can really pick up steam and pay off debt quickly.

That is the magic of the debt snowball method. Many people make the mistake of trying to spread out extra payments over all of their bills. This bill gets an extra $20, that bill gets an extra $15, this bill gets an extra $5, but the problem is you're not paying enough money to impact the collective interest you're paying on all of this debt. Once you're able to concentrate all of your energy, all of your focus, and all of your extra money to one item, you'll see mountains of debt chiseled away very quickly, you'll become your own sculpture, like Michelangelo, but with your own credit.

The debt snowball method isn't always the fastest way to eliminate debt, but what it does for most people is that it allows them to keep up the fight against bad debt. All too often, people get overwhelmed by debt and they stop, but with the debt snowball, the FOCUS glaring at just one item makes every amount of debt you have manageable, because now, you're not looking at a total number, you're just going after one.

Debt Avalanche

If the debt snowball for many is the most effective way to pay off the debt, the debt avalanche is definitely the most efficient. The debt avalanche has a completely different focus, as it targets the highest interest debt, no matter what. So if you have a $1,000 credit card with a low-interest rate and a $7,000 credit card with a high-interest rate, the debt avalanche is going to have you tackle the higher balance, because it has the highest interest rate.

The key to it is that it eliminates interest, therefore saving you as much money as you could manage, by paying more money into your debt avalanche. Like the debt snowball, after you've paid off one bill, you're going to roll over all extra payments, all the extra money, towards the second debt. According to the numbers, this method is going to be the most efficient, because unlike the debt snowball, where the focus is the smallest balance, eliminating high-interest debt allows you to flat out save more money.

The challenge with the debt avalanche is, if you need smaller wins, you might have to wait longer to see the results you're looking for. However, if you are an analytical and patient person, the debt avalanche is the way to go. Numbers don't lie and saving more money by eliminating high interest debt is ultimately going to be the fastest path to eliminating debt and the most effective way to becoming debt free.

Both of these methods are extremely effective and either one you commit to could have you ultimately debt free in a reasonable amount of time. The question is, are you a person who needs small victories, or are you willing to wait? If you're willing to wait, without a doubt, the debt avalanche is going to save you more money.

All the while, it may cost you a little more money but you're able to get those smaller victories and use them as fuel to keep on going, by all means, feel free to explore the debt snowball option. The ultimate goal is financial freedom and fortunately, there are different ways to get there.

I recommend the debt snowball for my clients because I want them to see results in the period of time we're contracted to work together. When that happens, the momentum I've been able to experience with them has just been phenomenal. It empowers them to go after one, then the other, and I see a difference in the way they deal with their money. The debt avalanche can have a similar impact. It's just a matter of knowing exactly which strategy fits you. Ultimately, if you want to eliminate debt and get on the path to financial freedom, start with one of these two methods. They will both improve your credit in the process.

Debt Collections:

A collection account can lead to a huge drop in your credit score. It could be the reason someone is denied for credit and ultimately makes obtaining credit more difficult. A collection happens when there is a severely past due debt that has been sold to a collection agency, or a collection agency has been hired to pursue a consumer for that debt. Satisfying a debt before it becomes a collection is preferred. Once it becomes a collection account, there are a number of negative impacts a consumer can face.

1. A significant drop in your credit score
2. It's an additional negative account being reported separately from the original creditor. Therefore, one negative account essentially splits and becomes two

negative accounts, one with the original creditor and one with the collection agency.

3. Persistent phone calls and collection attempts from collection agencies.
4. The debt collection business has had a reputation for less than stellar practices. Before you consider paying a collection company any money, there are a number of things to keep in mind:
5. You didn't sign any contract with the collection agency.
6. In order for them to collect from you, you have to admit the debt is yours.
7. They should provide proof you owe the debt.
8. They must have the “wet ink” contract from the original creditor to collect on any debt.

There is also a statute of limitations on legal action a collection company can take against you. If you have an old collection account, in many cases, it's better to not pay it at all, because it's going to be removed from your credit report after seven years. However, a collection agency won't be able to take any legal action against you after four to six years depending on your state. An example of why that matters is if you're closing on a home, and you have an old credit account on your credit report. Paying an old collection is going to cause your credit score to drop. Collection accounts hurt your credit most when they first appear on your credit. It’s impact is felt less and less over time. Paying off an old collection account is generating new activity on an old negative account. It’s like bringing up an old argument in a new conversation with your mate. If you can, in advance of getting approved for a mortgage, dispute any old collection items to have them removed from your credit report. You can do this through a traditional credit dispute letter, or a debt validation letter depending on how old the collection account is and the details on how it is reported.

Another thing to know is that collection agencies can't cross state lines. If you move to another state, old collection companies can't pursue you for a debt in the state you used to live in. They would have to, by law, sell your debt, or give the debt to another agency to collect in your state. Most won't do this because it costs time and money, and keeping in mind the four to six years statute of limitations, they probably have bigger fish to fry.

Collection accounts are a very important part of credit. If you fall on hard times and an item goes into collections, how you deal with it is very important. If it is a newer collection account, less than two to three years old, you would be best served to satisfy it if it can't be removed from your credit report. You do not want those to get in the way of a major purchase you may be considering. When negotiating with the collection company, keep in mind, it's all negotiable. There are five likely outcomes, let's go through which ones are the best and which ones are acceptable.

The best case scenario is getting the account removed with a settlement. You would negotiate with the debt collector to have the account deleted from your credit report, in exchange for paying a portion of the amount owed. This is the best case scenario and also known as a "Pay for Deletion."

Another Pay for Deletion outcome, which is the second-best outcome, is to have the account removed with the full payment. If you offer to pay the account in full in exchange for the collector deleting the account from your credit report, this is also a Pay for Deletion option. The difference is, if you can get them to satisfy it for less than you owe and still have it removed, that's the best possible outcome.

The third best option, or a satisfactory scenario, is to have it settled, and have it reported as paid in full. When you get the debt collector to agree to update the accounts as paid in full, the agreement should be in writing. Everything with the collection agency should be in writing.

A less favorable, but still acceptable outcome, is when you settle, but it's reported as settled. Financially settling a debt can be good for you, especially if you're tight on money. If you settle the amount and the collector accepts and updates your account as paid but settled, it's not the best but at least you saved some money. What's acceptable as well, is to pay the debt in full. After you pay the collection, make sure you keep the paperwork and proof of your payment and monitor your credit going forward just to make sure the collector made the appropriate updates.

These five means of negotiating your debt could help you to get rid of pesky collection agencies. Once those are in the rearview mirror, a consumer can take steps to start establishing positive credit.

As a credit professional, I see some people who have not fulfilled their purpose and destiny in life. They may have buried their dreams in debt and can’t move forward to the things they truly desire. They may believe that their low credit score equals low self-worth or an inability to do game changing things in life.

Despite our shortcomings and limitations, we are not defined by our mistakes. Mistakes are events and not a person. The great thing about the challenges that we create for ourselves is that we have the power to create the solution. Let's not die with our untapped potential, but leave it all on the playing field of life. Let's build legacies we can be proud to leave behind. Whether it's debt elimination or writing the next classic novel, we all can take some time to begin to FOCUS. It's in each and everyone one of us to follow one course until we're successful.

Jeanette did just that. In just two years she eliminated over $30,000 of her $80,000 in debt. She's used her income, her tax refunds, and money she generated from doing yard sales and other creative means to gain income to pay down her debt. Feeling empowered by her success and FOCUSed on maintaining her momentum, Jeanette will ultimately pay off all of her debt. For the first time in more than a decade, Jeanette is finally in control of her money and her future. As a result, Jeanette is preparing and planning to start her own business because she can focus on her future instead of being trapped in a debt-ridden past. This is the blueprint she followed and one you can follow to do the same.

Your Blueprint:

- Collect all of your statements for your credit payments.
- Use a debit card instead of a credit card to stop accumulating debt.
- List all credit debt from the smallest balance to the largest balance.

- Dedicate the money remaining from your monthly budget to eliminate the smallest credit balance.
- Rollover the minimum payment and surplus from your budget to eliminate the second smallest credit balance.
- Continue to rollover minimum payments and budget surplus to eliminate all debt.
- Calculate how long it would take to pay off all of your debt as the Debt Snowball gets bigger and bigger.

Chapter FIVE

Knowing and Understanding the Building Codes

"There is a great difference between knowing and understanding; you can know a lot about something and not really understand it."

~ Charles Franklin Kettering

At one of our local Real Estate Investment Association meetings, I bumped into my friend Peter. Always happy to see him, I said, "Hey Peter, how's it going?" Standing there with a long face and sad eyes, he replied, "TERRIBLE!"

Working on his third fix and flip deal, Peter went on to explain how the code enforcer caused him to stop construction on his property. Now faced with having to pull the proper property permits along with the associated fees, this was costing Peter time and money. He was sidelined because he didn't follow the appropriate building codes.

Like Peter, how much is not knowing the credit building codes costing you? The building codes are established to reduce variability and establish credibility in the foundation and structure of the property. Knowing and understanding how to use the codes for credit does the same thing for your ability to get financing for your goals.

The credit laws govern all parties involved in the credit process. Consumers need to know the laws to avoid being impacted by predatory practices by creditors and the credit bureaus. The credit bureaus need to keep in line with what information they can report and what must be removed from a credit report. Creditors have to follow proper collection strategies to pursue delinquent borrowers. These are the rules. Know them, and use them to your advantage to get to the credit that will open up doors for you.

The Fair Credit Reporting Act

The Fair Credit Reporting Act (**FCRA**) is the chief legislative policy that governs your credit. The purpose of the FCRA is to promote fairness, accuracy, and privacy of consumer credit being reported. This law was enacted in 1970 and is enforced by the Federal Trade Commission (FTC), and the Consumer Financial Protection Bureau. According to a study done by the FTC in 2015, 23% of consumers reported inaccuracies on their credit report. The Fair Credit Reporting Act allows consumers to dispute inaccurate items on their credit report to ensure they are not being negatively impacted by these errors. The credit bureaus have thirty days from the time of receipt of any dispute to investigate the disputed item. If the investigation of a dispute isn't concluded within that time frame, the item must be removed from a consumer's credit profile in accordance with the law.

When negative items are reported, the impact on a consumer's life can be significant. Being that it can affect so many areas of life, the time limitation on credit events is one of the most powerful measures the FCRA enacted to protect consumers. According to this law, negative items reported to credit agencies can only be reported for seven years. After which, it must be removed from the credit report. The exception to this rule is bankruptcy. Bankruptcy can be reported for up to ten years. What this does is give people hope. Just because someone may have experienced a credit hardship in the past, doesn't mean it should be a life sentence. Many Americans who go through credit challenges get stuck with bad credit because they don't know there's a chance at redemption.

The Fair and Accurate Credit Transactions Act

The FACT Act (Fair and Accurate Credit Transactions Act) is an addendum to the FCRA passed in 2003. Under this law, consumers are entitled to get a free copy of their credit report each year. According to this law, consumers are able to review their credit reports for educational and informational purposes without the potential negative impact of a credit inquiry. These laws give clients the power to demand the accuracy and fairness of every item reported to their credit profile. Understanding the basics of these laws can help consumers be more empowered to get information about their credit.

Credit Bureaus

Credit bureaus are gigantic multinational, multi-billion dollar corporations with so much power over your lives. Why is that? Well, they're the ones who report if and report when you have made your payments to your creditors. They also report other personal information about you and many of those things show up on your credit report. If they make a mistake in their reporting, it could impact you by causing you to be denied for a mortgage, a loan, or even a job. As big as they are, the big three credit bureaus, Experian, Equifax, and Transunion are all subject to credit laws.

One of their chief responsibilities is to only report accurate information. That means if you find an address that's not yours you can dispute it and have it removed, if there is no evidence you resided there. That is the same for a collection account or a late payment on a credit report that doesn't belong to you. You can dispute any of the information being reported on your credit report. As long as the information cannot be verified and validated, it has to be removed.

A common error causing significant issues for consumers, is an incorrect spelling of a name, or a suffix like Jr. or Sr. Unfortunately, many children have a parent's debt reported to their credit because of the similarity in the name. With proof of identity, a Jr. can have Sr.'s negative credit items removed from their credit so they don't have to carry the burden of a parent's debt. This also happens with an incorrect date of birth or the wrong social security number. To remedy these issues, the law offers consumers the chance to send in documented evidence along with a dispute letter to have those issues corrected.

Collection accounts are some of the most disputed items. That happens because the company calling or contacting you by mail to collect on the debt is not the company you had an agreement with. Often, in the process of them acquiring personal information, they may not have the necessary information or documentation to validate the debt of the person they are pursuing. In many cases, they are only able to continue their pursuit because a consumer gives them information they didn't have or confirms the debt is theirs. Unscrupulous debt collectors are less concerned with the debt being accurate than they are with collecting money on a debt. The fact that they can report it to your credit gives them leverage. By knowing how to use the law, you can force a debt collector to prove they have the required information to hold you accountable to a debt.

An accurate credit report is important because mistakes can directly impact a credit score, or leave consumers open to bigger issues. When information is reported inaccurately, it can get intertwined with someone else's information, which could lead to items not belonging to you being attributed to you. So one inaccuracy could lead to other inaccuracies that can hurt you.

In that time, the item being disputed must be removed unless properly verified or validated. You have the right to escalate the dispute if credit bureaus do not respond in time or if they deny your claim without providing adequate proof it's accurate.

As previously mentioned, the statute of limitations for negative items to be reported on credit is seven years. If there is debt still reporting after the allowable time frame, you can use the dispute process to have that debt removed. Savvy debt collectors can get an old debt to restart the seven-year clock all over by having you acknowledge a debt over the phone or in writing. Beware of these techniques because once you verbally acknowledge a debt, you have put your credit back on the hook.

According to the Consumer Financial Protection Bureau, 76% of credit reports contain some form of inaccuracy. It could be a big inaccuracy, like a late payment that wasn't yours, or it could be something small, like an "A" that's missing from your last name. Either way, check your credit report so you can make sure every detail that belongs there is there and every detail that doesn't is removed.

Taking the time to ensure your credit report is fully accurate and optimized could save you a lot of money and pain. For people who haven't checked their credit and maybe have been the victims of identity theft, they could be building up debt without even knowing it. Checking your credit report gives you an opportunity to put your credit back in your hands. Once you know what is there, you get to be intentional about what your plans are for your credit.

Yes, the credit bureaus are powerful but when it comes to your credit, you have even more power. Experian, Equifax, and Transunion can only report the information that's accurate. If they do not, you can fix it. If you are late, they could only report that because you missed a payment. If you set a plan for yourself and stay committed to your goals, you can make sure your credit score is a reflection of your growth and not your deficiencies. Eventually, you will be able to access all of the funding you need for your house, your car, or for a big project.

The Fair Debt Collection Practices Act

One of the best parts about the Fair Debt Collection Practices Act (**FDCPA**) is it gives you the power to demand a collection agency verifies your debt. What that means is before you accept any debt and acknowledge it, you want to send in a letter asking them to verify the debt is indeed yours. You are putting the burden of proof on them to prove they have the required information from the original creditor. They must be able to produce the original amount of the loan, the original creditor, their address, and the "wet ink" contract from the original debt. If they're not able to do that within thirty days, by law, they have to remove that item from your credit and stop collection activities.

This is how you could actually use this law in your favor every single time an item comes up on your credit report you cannot be sure is verifiable. In addition, collection agencies just can't call you whenever they want. They're mandated to only call you between 8:00 AM to 9:00 PM. If you've experienced getting calls early in the morning or after 9 pm, there are legal actions you can take to protect yourself.

I received a collection call one morning while I was running. It definitely was not my debt, but after showing them I not only knew the law but understood it, they were very apologetic and I never heard from them again.

If I had chosen to, I could have sued them. If you sue on the grounds of them calling outside of mandated timeframes, you could actually earn a $1,000 judgment against the collection companies. Additionally, if you work overnights and sleep during the day, debt collectors won't be able to call you during those times once you establish that with them.

You are also protected against abusive language or profanity during a collection call. If that happens, you're also entitled to sue for a monetary reward. There are a number of rules debt collectors must abide by. Any debt collector calling you has to present their information of who they are, what company they represent, and who the original creditor on your debt is. Beyond that, they're not allowed to report any inaccurate information.

Collection agencies only hurt themselves if they are no longer able to contact you, or worse, have monetary consequences for mistakes they make in pursuing you for a debt. No one ever wants to deal with a collection agency, am I right? If you are ever in a position where you are getting these calls though, you want to know what to do to make sure you are protected. In the event you are being harassed by a collection agency, use the Fair Debt Collection Practices Act in your favor. Report them to the Federal Trade Commission. If it can be proven you were called at the wrong time or you were a victim of abusive language or your information was shared with parties that didn't need to know any of your business, you could win monetary damages of up to $1,000. Sure, it's not a lot of money, but it's a slap on the wrist that could at least get them to stop calling you and probably give you the money to actually pay off some debt.

Do you think you would have been more empowered to deal with collection agency calls if you knew and understood the laws better? No matter which way you answer, knowing is half the battle. With an understanding, you are just one step closer to building excellent credit.

Statute of Limitations

Another area where a collection agency could find themselves in trouble is if you send in a “Cease and Desist” letter. If you state they can no longer call you, or write to you, they will be punished if they do. They would be in violation of the Fair Debt Collection Practices Act. If a collection agency no longer has the ability to call or write to you, they are more than likely to file a judgment against you. If they want to collect on a debt, that is pretty much the only option they are left with to pursue you for the debt. Now, if this is an older debt, there is a statute of limitations in every state prohibiting the amount of time any collection agency, or creditor, could pursue you legally for a debt.

They could still report it to your credit report for up to seven years but they won't have the ability to file a judgment and demand you make that payment, depending on the statute of limitations for the state in which the debt originated. In Delaware, it's as little as three years, but most states are five to six years. Research exactly what the statute of limitations is if you have any older debt, so you could be prepared and know if that statute of limitations has passed. If so, you can submit a cease and desist letter and there's nothing they can do about it. Prior to that point, you want to be very careful and make sure not to leave yourself open to having a judgment filed against you.

Collection accounts can happen. Debt collection happens. However, if you deal with them the right way, you could put yourself in a position where your credit avoids the most severe impact because you know how to address it and get the best results, even in a bad situation.

Statute of Limitation by State:

State	Oral	Written	Promissory	Open
Alabama	6	6	6	3
Alaska	6	6	3	3
Arizona	3	5	6	3
Arkansas	3	6	3	3
California	2	4	4	4
Colorado	6	6	6	6
Connecticut	3	6	6	3
Delaware	3	3	3	4

Florida	4	5	5	4
Georgia	4	6	6	6
Hawaii	6	6	6	6
Idaho	4	5	5	5
Illinois	5	10	10	5
Indiana	6	10	10	6
Iowa	5	10	5	5
Kansas	3	5	5	3
Kentucky	5	10	15	5
Louisiana	10	10	10	3

Maine	6	6	6	6
Maryland	3	3	6	3
Massachusetts	6	6	6	6
Michigan	6	6	6	6
Minnesota	6	6	6	6
Mississippi	3	3	3	3
Missouri	5	10	10	5
Montana	5	8	8	5
Nebraska	4	5	5	4
Nevada	4	6	3	4

New Hampshire	3	3	6	3
New Jersey	6	6	6	6
New Mexico	4	6	6	4
New York	6	6	6	6
North Carolina	3	3	5	3
North Dakota	6	6	6	6
Ohio	15	15	15	6
Oklahoma	3	5	5	3
Oregon	6	6	6	6
Pennsylvania	4	4	4	4

Rhode Island	10	10	10	10
South Carolina	3	3	3	3
South Dakota	3	6	6	6
Tennessee	6	6	6	6
Texas	4	4	4	4
Utah	4	6	6	4
Vermont	6	6	5	3
Virginia	3	5	6	3
Washington	3	6	6	3
West Virginia	5	10	6	5

Wisconsin	6	6	10	6
Wyoming	8	10	10	8

Your Blueprint:

- All bad credit has an expiration date. Dispute any negative items still on your credit report seven years after the last activity, unless it's a bankruptcy.
- Challenge all collections to provide the wet ink, original contract proving you owe the debt.
- Find out the statute of limitations in your state for pursuing you with debt collection.
- The FCRA gives you the right to dispute any inaccurate, unverifiable, or outdated information on your credit report.
- Arm yourself with information regarding the credit laws, then apply the information and use it properly for more understanding.

Chapter SIX

Brick by Brick

"A successful man is one who can lay a firm foundation with the bricks others have thrown at him."

~ David Brinkley

As a young man growing up in Philadelphia, Will Smith was given a big chore. His father ordered him and his brother to build a wall. They had never built anything before, so this task of building a wall seemed impossible. Still, that was his job and it had to be completed. Will Smith says he learned a valuable lesson we all can benefit from.

He said, "You don't set out to build a wall. You say, I'm going to lay this brick as perfectly as a brick can be laid. You do that every single day and soon enough you'll have a wall."

He credits this life lesson with the success he's achieved as a rapper, actor, and overall motivational figure. Will's words can serve as encouragement as we seek to uncover a path to paying off student loans within this chapter and we'll do so, brick by brick.

When mortgage bankers qualify borrowers for a home loan, they look at their debt-to-income ratio as a core factor. It will determine how much a borrower will be able to qualify for. Lending criteria has been adjusted to make it easier for people with student loan debt to qualify for a loan, but with student loans in the high five figures or six figure ranges, there's only so much that can be done. Because of this, mortgage bankers send clients to me who are saddled with more student loan debt than can justify them getting a mortgage. Some cases are more severe than others, but my advice whether the debt is large or huge is the same. Let's take it brick by brick, step-by-step, and soon enough you will buy your home and pay off your student loan debt.

Understandably, people who have gotten themselves into large, or huge amounts of student loan debt often use adjectives like overwhelmed, or helpless. The truth is, student loan debt is some of the best debt you can have. It offers opportunities to have it forgiven, have late payment history reversed, and payment plans reduced by what you can afford. Laws have been put in place to make the student loan repayment process less painful. If you understand the best way to make the process work for you, you can save money and years of payments by taking the right steps.

Higher education offers an opportunity to expand employment options, learn about yourself, and connect with people who can be lifelong influences. It's almost a rite of passage in our country and unfortunately, it comes at a steep cost. The class of 2017 had an average of $39,400 in student loan debt. Student loan debt is at a crisis point in our economy. We have reached $1.5 trillion in student loan debt, which has surpassed the totals for credit card and auto financing debt. With around 20 million students expected to enroll in American colleges in 2018, expect these figures to continue to skyrocket at an alarming rate. The impact of this enormous debt can have a crippling effect on finances.

My client, Terry-Ann once told me, "I wanted to call you months ago to work on my credit, but I knew with all this student loan debt, it was pointless. I won't be able to buy a house. I won't be able to do anything financially because I'm just suffocating under all of these student loans."

Many Americans feel the same way, Terry-Ann isn't the only one. It's not all bad though. There are many options to help you live your life with student loan debt. For Federal student loans, there are a number of programs available to help borrowers with different levels of challenges with their loans. Even mortgage banks have made it more feasible for student loan holders to be able to get a house. To qualify for a mortgage, lenders are using 1% of the total student loan debt as a payment to qualify for a mortgage. That ratio gives student loan holders the opportunity to buy houses even though the total student loan debt is substantial.

Where to Start:

There are so many different student loans and student loan repayment options. You may have a Perkins loan, a Stafford loan, a private loan, a Parent PLUS, to name a few. Some loans are subsidized and others are unsubsidized. With all of these possibilities, just finding out what kind of loan you have is an important task. You can call your student loan servicer, and all of your Federal student loan information can be found online. The National Student Loan Data Systems website, www.nslds.ed.gov is the starting place for all Federal student loan information. When you log in to this website, you'll be given the amounts you owe, your loan servicer, the interest rates, and whether a loan is subsidized or not. Empowered with this information, you will be able to create a game plan to navigate financial hardships and enter into the best student loan repayment and loan forgiveness programs available. While student loans give many borrowers a feeling of hopelessness because of the sheer amounts owed, they offer flexible options that can lead borrowers out of student loan related credit challenges.

The Interest Trap

When discussing compound interest, Benjamin Franklin once said, "Money makes money. And the money that money makes, makes money." Unfortunately, student loan borrowers are on the wrong side of that equation.

Lisa's Story

Lisa came to me with a burning desire to buy a home and a credit report full of student loan debt. She graduated from college eight years previously; however, she'd been able to avoid making payments on her student loans through different hardship programs. She'd participated in a deferment, forbearance, and she was currently in a loan rehabilitation program to get her delinquent student loans back in good standing. After eight years, Lisa's total student loan balance was

$11,000. On a scale of one to horrible, she was in fair shape in terms of the total she had to repay. However, when she told me the initial loan amount was $6,000, reality sunk in. She had almost doubled the amount of student loan debt she originally borrowed. The worst part about it is she now had to pay interest on top of the compounded interest accruing on her loan.

Benjamin Franklin would have been proud if she had been able to generate such a positive return in that period of time. The amount of compounded interest that can build on a student loan is often exorbitant. When you are given a chance not to make payments, it's vital to ask questions and understand the details of your student loan and the repercussions of your choices. Deferments and other hardship programs offer immediate relief from payments but with the interest still being tallied, it becomes a short-term gain for long-term pain in many instances.

Lisa's Blueprint

Lisa found herself in a hole. The first thing she had to do was stop digging the hole. Having interest compound on top of interest would make paying off her loan impossible. The way she had to stop the cycle was by finding out her loan repayment options. Deferments and forbearance has its place, but when they hinder you more than they help, it's time for other options. In Lisa's case, she had to contact her loan servicer to find out the right repayment options. When a borrower is facing financial hardship, Income Driven Repayment plans can be the perfect solution.

Since they are based on your current income, borrowers are able to get loan payments that reflect their financial situation. It is not uncommon for loan servicers to grant borrowers payments that can be $20, $10, $1, or as low as $0. Lisa was able to stop going backwards on her loan repayment by getting a plan that gave her a very low, very affordable payment while having payments that would go towards her loan forgiveness schedule. While the balance still went up for the unsubsidized portion of her loan, with 120 consecutive payments her remaining balance could be forgiven since she was an employee of a Non-profit organization.

Deferment:

People invest ten to hundreds of thousands of dollars to pursue higher education with the hopes of landing a high-paying job. A day out of college, most people don't find themselves in their dream career. For most, it takes time to find a job, not to mention their dream job. That's why students are given a six to nine month grace period after they graduate, drop below half-time enrollment, or drop out before payments are required to be made on most student loans.

This time frame is called a "deferment" period. A deferment can also happen when a borrower is facing financial hardship. In the event of unemployment, you can have your Federal student loans deferred for up to three years. You can also be eligible for up to a three-year deferment if you are an active duty member in the Military. The reason why a deferment is such a beneficial tool is it does not negatively impact your credit. If you went three years without making payments on any other loan, your credit would be damaged and you would be facing collections. Federal student loans make it so this grace period helps people through the most challenging financial times.

Forbearance

If you do not qualify for a deferment, forbearance would be the next best option. A forbearance temporarily allows you to stop making monthly payments to your loan servicer. While borrowers will receive relief from the monthly payment, the interest will continue to accrue. Forbearances are given in 12 month periods. It can be renewed for up to 3 years.

Subsidized Student Loans

Subsidized loans are Federal student loans the government pays interest on while you are in school or in the midst of a deferment. Direct loans and Perkins Loans are primary forms of Federal loans the government subsidizes. These are loans issued to undergraduate borrowers.

Unsubsidized Student Loans

One of the biggest negative elements of student loans is the impact of unsubsidized loans on student loan balances. During a deferment, being able to keep afloat financially is the priority. However, the longer you don't pay on an unsubsidized student loan, the more money you will have to pay over time.

Vivian had just gotten a new job after two years of unemployment and underemployment. She had to live off of credit cards and was unable to meet a lot of her financial obligations. Her new job would give her the financial foundation to be able to catch up on her bills, pay down her credit cards, and start making her student loan payments again. When she went into her deferment, her student loan balance was only $14,000. However, when she called to start her payments back, her balance had risen to over $19,000.

In such a short period of time, her balance had increased by almost 50%. The worst part about it is that her loan had capitalized, which means the interest was added to the principal balance of the loan. Instead of paying interest on the remaining $14,000, she would now have to pay interest on her new $19,000 balance. This is why unsubsidized loans can be so dangerous. At least a portion of most student loan packages will be unsubsidized. They are very beneficial loans in most cases, but compared to Subsidized Loans, they are less attractive.

Knowing more about your student loans can allow you to focus on classes, papers, and enjoying campus life. The difference between unsubsidized and subsidized loans can be tens of thousands of dollars. These are the loan programs the government subsidizes during deferment:

- Direct Subsidized Loans
- Direct Consolidation Loans (a portion is subsidized)
- Federal Stafford Loans
- FFEL Consolidation Loans (a portion can be subsidized)
- Federal Perkins Loans

These are some of the loans available for undergraduate studies. Parent Plus loans and student loans for graduate studies will not be subsidized. When in need of a deferment or forbearance, find out what portion of your payment is interest. To avoid having your loan capitalize and get bigger and bigger with time, borrowers can pay the interest portion of the loan. While a borrower's credit will be protected during a deferment or forbearance, financial troubles can be pushed down the road as a result of larger balances that will have to be paid off. Many people feel like their student loan debt is insurmountable. That feeling can be justified when you see your balance going up instead of down. Being proactive about the interest payments on unsubsidized loans can save a lot of money and time on your student loan.

While not every aspect of federal student loans is positive, they offer flexibility no other loan programs do. The ability to take a break when things get hard makes student loans particularly attractive. If you are in a tight place financially, take advantage of this security blanket. When times are tough, it is a tremendous benefit to know your credit won't be damaged and you will be given the chance to get your finances in order.

Another element of Federal student loans that can be a huge saving grace is the Loan Rehabilitation program.

Loan Rehabilitation:

One of the key factors that makes student loan debt easier to deal with is the way they handle late payments and default. When a borrower misses multiple consecutive payments, the loan can go into default. This is a collection status in which a third party agency can be used to call and pursue the borrower for delinquent payments. The impact of a default can be devastating to a credit profile and hinder a borrower from being able to attain credit or additional student loans. A collection status can be achieved with any kind of credit. The difference with Federal student loans is borrowers can enter a payment program to get out of default. This program is called the Loan Rehabilitation program.

Rodney's Story

Rodney was getting ready to bid on the biggest contract he ever had for his construction company. The challenge was he needed to be able to finance the equipment to complete the project if he won the contract. His credit score was 489, and he was in deep student loan debt. There was no way he'd be able to get credit to pay for the necessary materials unless he did something about his credit. While he had a few minor issues on his credit, his student loans were in really bad shape. Rodney's student loan issues started when his business hit a rocky patch. He was not getting enough contracts to pay his mortgage, car note, and his student loans. So he made the choice to stop paying his student loans. Now, years later, his student loans were in default and his credit was suffering for it. He didn't have much time but wanted to try with everything he had to take his business to the next level. If this had been a car loan or a credit card, Rodney would have been out of luck and out of time. Fortunately, Federal student loans are very forgiving.

Rodney's Blueprint

Rodney started by looking up his student loan details online. There, he saw what he owed and who he owed it to. He called up his student loan servicer and requested a Loan Rehabilitation. The Loan Rehabilitation program allows borrowers with student loans that are in default to work their way out of default with a nine-month payment plan. In just nine months, borrowers can get their student loans out of default and the loan servicer will change the negative payment history on the loan to positive. The impact that can have on a credit report is amazing. Rodney had three years of delinquent payments wiped clean in just nine months.

Actually, in Rodney's case, the payment history was re-reported as positive in just six months. His credit went from being in the 400s to the high 600s as a result of the Loan Rehabilitation program and his commitment to taking the appropriate steps to build his credit in other places. He won the contract and was able to get the funding he needed to get the equipment to complete the project. This was a transformative process that changed the trajectory of his business and his life.

Rodney's story is not unique. The Loan Rehabilitation program is a one of a kind resolution. It helps people who have negative history with their student loans get a second chance to get it right. The credit score increases as a result of this program can be hundreds of points depending on the credit profile. Borrowers who had feelings of hopelessness can see their student loan situations turned right side up within a matter of months. Whether someone had been in default for six months or six years, this program can be the game changer that opens the door for more opportunities.

How does the Loan Rehabilitation program work? A student loan can go into default after about nine months without a payment being received by the loan servicer. While in default, borrowers would not be eligible for further financial aid for school until the default is paid off or entered into a suitable repayment plan. Borrowers can also have their wages garnished and their tax refund seized in lieu of the default. As bad as one's financial situation may be, bankruptcy would not eliminate a Federal student loan debt. That's why loan rehabilitation is such an empowering policy.

To start the process of getting loan rehabilitation, get your loan information. Once you get the information about your default, you can call your loan servicer. Unlike most bills, when an item is in collections, you can still communicate with the loan servicer to create a payment plan and work out a resolution. You will be required to make nine consecutive payments to get out of default. Once your loan is taken out of default, your loan will be reinstated and the default and delinquent payments will be removed from your credit report.

Consolidation:

Another resolution that can help you to get out of default and improve the reporting of delinquencies to credit is by doing a consolidation. Consolidation allows you to have all of your student loans put into one loan. With a consolidation, instead of making numerous payments to each student loan you have, you'll be responsible for one payment for all of the loans.

Consolidation offers a number of benefits. In addition to giving a borrower just one payment, they can also offer an opportunity for variable rate loans to be converted to fixed-rate loans. Borrowers will also usually end up with a lower monthly payment. Loan consolidations are amortized to be paid off in thirty years. By spreading out the time to pay off the loan, most borrowers experience a significant decrease in payments. You can also get access to additional payment plans and loan forgiveness programs by doing a consolidation.

A consolidation can give a borrower a lower payment, but will start a new thirty-year term loan once it starts. That means more payments and more interest. If you owe interest at the time of the consolidation, the loan is capitalized, so the interest is added to the principal balance. So not only will you be paying more interest for ten years, but you'll also have to pay interest on top of the interest built up on your loan.

One of the biggest things to be aware of during a consolidation is the fact you can lose all benefits such as payment reduction or credit toward a Public Service Loan Forgiveness program. The time and money that had been invested in other payment plans will be lost once the consolidation goes through. You do have the option to exclude loans from your Direct Consolidation Loan. For example, if you have a Direct Loan on which you have been making payments towards Public Service Loan Forgiveness and other Federal Student loans, you can do a Direct Consolidation Loan, and not include the loans that are on track to be forgiven. A Direct Consolidation Loan pays off all loans that are in the consolidation. All terms, benefits, and history associated with those loans are no longer active. They are closed and your new Direct Consolidation Loan is opened.

A Direct Consolidation Loan can be a great solution for your student loan issues. The important thing to know is that it is not for everyone and every situation. Like other student loan payment options, it offers flexibility that can make it a net benefit. For example, while they are scheduled to be paid off in thirty years, loan balances can be forgiven if a borrower does the consolidation with a payment plan. These payment plans make you eligible for loan forgiveness in twenty years, or even in ten years through the Public Service Loan Forgiveness. If you currently are in a Public Service Loan Forgiveness program, you would want to avoid a consolidation for that loan. Being strategic about your approach to loan consolidation can put you in position to have a lower monthly payment, just one payment, and the possibility of having loans forgiven years before the scheduled payoff time. If your student loans are eligible for a Direct Consolidation Loan, speak with your loan servicer to find out if this could be the best option for you.

These Loans Are Eligible for a Direct Consolidation Loan:

Most federal student loans, including the following, are eligible for consolidation:

- Subsidized Federal Stafford Loans
- Unsubsidized and Subsidized Federal Stafford Loans
- PLUS loans from the Federal Family Education Loan (FFEL) Program

- Supplemental Loans for Students
- Federal Perkins Loans
- Nursing Student Loans
- Nurse Faculty Loans
- Health Education Assistance Loans
- Health Professions Student Loans
- Loans for Disadvantaged Students
- Direct Subsidized Loans
- Direct Unsubsidized Loans
- Direct PLUS Loans
- FFEL Consolidation Loans and Direct Consolidation Loans (only under certain conditions)
- Federal Insured Student Loans
- Guaranteed Student Loans
- National Direct Student Loans
- National Defense Student Loans
- Parent Loans for Undergraduate Students
- Auxiliary Loans to Assist Students

Payment Plans:

The best resource to get information about student loans is www.studentaid.ed.gov. Here, you can find out about all of your options with your student loans. This site goes into great detail about all of the payment plans available to borrowers with a variety of loan scenarios. We will go into more detail about the payment plans that impact the most borrowers, but there are more plans depending on individual situations. When people start paying their student loans, they are put on the Standard Plan. They can enroll in other plans that offer faster routes to paying off student loans. The Standard Plan is amortized to be paid off in ten years. The interest rates are relatively low but paying off tens or hundreds of thousands of dollars in 10 years can become challenging—especially when just starting out in a career or finding a career path. Borrowers often negotiate out of Standard Plans when they face financial hardship or if they apply for Public Service Loan Forgiveness.

To make it easier for students to payoff student loan debt, Federal Student Loans offer a number of payment options including Extended, Graduated, and Income Driven Plans. Each speaks to a different need and knowing who they serve and how they work will help borrowers get to the finish line in the fastest time while paying the least amount of interest they can. If you need a lower payment, one of the easiest options to get is an Extended Plan. It allows you to pay your loans off in up to twenty-five years. By giving borrowers more time to pay, the monthly payments are lower. The eligibility for each of these plans including the Extended Plan varies, based on the loan type and amount owed. The details of each of the payment options can be found in the resource section of this book.

To get an Extended Plan, you must have over $30,000 outstanding for your FFEL Loan or Direct Loan. This loan option is usually less than the Standard Loan payment and Graduated Loan payments. Graduated Loans start off lower than most Standard Loans and the payments increase over time with the expectation of increased income and the ability to pay more. Graduated payments set the expectation, the loan will be paid off in ten years like a traditional Standard Loan, but it does give up to thirty years with a Direct Consolidation Loan.

The most popular repayment options are Income-Driven Repayment Plans. These programs are based on a borrower's income and family size. If your income is low enough, you can even qualify for a $0.00/monthly payment.

Stephanie's Story:

Stephanie is a go-getter. When she came to me, she felt like her student loans were standing in the way of everything she wanted to accomplish in her life. She had her Master's degree but she owed so much she figured she would never pay off her student loan debt. Her income was also so low she questioned the investment she made into a college education. Her debt compared to her income was so high that not only was she worried about her student loans but also her car note, credit cards, and keeping a roof over her head.

I worked with her through the process of getting a payment plan and when her file was reviewed and approved, she ended up with a five dollar payment. Five dollars a month! Her payment was so low she could not believe it.

This is what's available with the various Income-Driven Repayment Plans. Another reason why the Income Driven Plan is so vital is that borrowers are required to be in one of these plans in order to qualify for Public Service Loan Forgiveness. We are going to look at four of the payment plans. Each one offers something different so more people can experience the option that is right for them.

Revised Pay As You Earn (REPAYE)

The Revised Pay As You Earn (**REPAYE**) program is the newest student loan repayment plan launched by the U.S. Department of Education in 2015. All Direct Subsidized and Unsubsidized Federal student loans are eligible for this program. It is an expansion on the Pay As You Earn (**PAYE**) program and does more to accommodate more borrowers. One of the biggest factors making this program the best option for many candidates is they don't have to wait for debt-to-income ratios to reach a crisis level before they are eligible. People of all income levels are eligible for the REPAYE plan. Payments can be as low as $0.00 a month for this plan.

While paying $0.00 won't pay your loan off, ever, the remaining balance of student loans for undergraduate studies could be eligible for loan forgiveness. Since this is based on income and family size, a low payment amount allows borrowers the time to recover from financial hardships. When a borrower generates more income, the loan payments will increase accordingly. For those applying for Public Service Loan Forgiveness, this payment plan is one of the best routes to get there.

Pay As You Earn (PAYE)

Many of the key factors in the REPAYE plan are true for the PAYE program. One factor the PAYE plan considers is when loans were taken out. To be eligible for this plan, you must be a new borrower on or after Oct. 1, 2007 and must have received a disbursement of a Direct Loan on or after Oct. 1, 2011. For people who amassed their student loans before

2007, they would not be able to get relief from this program. For those who do qualify, they are only required to pay up to 10% of their discretionary income.

Like the REPAYE plan, payments can go as low as $0.00 a month to accommodate clients in tough financial conditions. With large amounts of student loans and stronger income, they won't be asked to pay a large percentage of their income to their student loan servicers with this plan. Whether with high or low income, having high debt compared to income is a qualifying factor. Direct Subsidized and Unsubsidized loans, Direct Plus loans (made to students), and Direct Consolidation loans (restrictions apply) are eligible. This payment plan is so popular because it offers the lowest monthly payments compared to other programs and similar to the REPAYE plan. Since the payment is so low, you will usually end up paying more than the Standard Repayment Plan over the course of your loan.

For my clients looking to apply for student loan forgiveness, I recommend attempting to qualify for the REPAYE or the PAYE repayment plan. These are the most affordable paths to PSLF. Any amount forgiven through these Federal loan programs can be considered as income, requiring you to be subject to paying taxes on the income. For those with large sums of loans forgiven, it could turn into a tax burden. Speak with your loan servicer to be prepared for this possibility.

Income Based Repayment Plan (IBR)

Each of these payment plans offer some of the same benefits. Namely, a lower payment than the Standard

Repayment Plan. The Income Based Repayment (**IBR**) plan differs from the REPAYE and PAYE plans because the required payment is up to 15% of the borrower's discretionary income compared to the 10% required for the REPAYE and PAYE plans. IBR does help a group of borrowers that do not qualify for the REPAYE and PAYE plans. Subsidized and Unsubsidized Stafford Loan recipients are eligible for Income-Based Repayment but not all of these Unsubsidized loans are eligible for the REPAYE or PAYE. The IBR plan also accommodates all PLUS loans made out to students. With the REPAYE and PAYE, only Direct PLUS loans qualify.

To be eligible, you must have a high debt-to-income ratio. Loan servicers often offer IBR plans before they offer the other lower payment options, in order to make more money. The benefit the IBR plan holds is that it will help you to pay your loans off faster than you would if you had a lower payment. Based on a borrower's financial stability, that may be a better option for some. It will cost you less than the Standard Repayment Plan on a monthly basis, but cost more over the life of the loan.

Income Contingent Repayment Plan (ICR)

The ICR Plan is the most expensive of the payment plans so far. However, it serves a major demographic that the other loan programs exclude. The parents who took out loans for their children to go to school can get relief through this program. The ICR plan's payment is either 20% of a borrower's discretionary income or the amount you would pay on a repayment plan with a fixed payment over twelve years, adjusted according to your income. The payment would be the lesser of these two options. Unlike the other repayment plans, you don't have to demonstrate financial hardship to qualify for this plan.

Your income will still drive the repayment amount, so over time, a borrower can end up with a higher payment than the Standard Repayment Plan. The payment plan will start out lower than a Standard Plan but if a borrower significantly increases their income over the twelve-year repayment time, the payment can be higher. For borrowers who would like a lower payment but don't want their loans to linger for the next twenty years, this is a great option. It also can be used for Parent PLUS Loans. Parent borrowers can access this plan by consolidating their Parent PLUS Loans into a Direct Consolidation Loan. Even though the loan can be paid off in twelve years, ICR is still an option for loan forgiveness.

Payment plans have been developed to help borrowers in a myriad of financial situations. The common ground all of these programs offer is the opportunity to save money from what the standard ten-year repayment option would be. Your loan type, financial situation, income, and family size will ultimately determine which repayment plan will fit your life and finances best. Generally, the lower the payment, the longer it will take for you to pay off a loan. Also, with more time to pay a loan, the more interest will be paid.

When settling on the right payment plan for yourself, consider the short-term and long-term impact of your decision. A REPAYE plan may give a borrower the lowest payment, but the ICR will have a borrower pay less interest. Many people faced with a choice would go after the lowest payment option.

This option could be good for a borrower today but when they have a loan balance in eighteen years, while others have paid their loans off, could one feel differently? Every borrower won't qualify for the same payment plan, but find out which ones you do qualify for and decide the best option based on all the factors—not just the payment. All of these repayment plans can help you get loan forgiveness. Having a strategy and a game plan will help you make the most beneficial choice providing you the best repayment plan that works for your life and finances.

Income-Driven Repayment Plan Charts:

Income-Driven Repayment Plan	Payment Amount
REPAYE Plan	Generally 10 percent of your discretionary income.
PAYE Plan	Generally 10 percent of your discretionary income but never more than the 10-year Standard Repayment Plan amount
IBR Plan	Generally 10 percent of your discretionary income if you're a new borrower on or after July 1, 2014*, but never more than the 10-year Standard Repayment Plan amount Generally 15 percent of your discretionary income if you're not a new borrower on or after July 1,

	2014, but never more than the 10-year Standard Repayment Plan amount
ICR Plan	The lesser of the following: 20 percent of your discretionary income or what you would pay on a repayment plan with a fixed payment over the course of 12 years, adjusted according to your income

Income-Driven Repayment Plan	Repayment Period
REPAYE Plan	20 years if all loans you are repaying under the plan were received for undergraduate study 25 years if any loans you're repaying under the plan were received for graduate or professional study
PAYE Plan	20 years
IBR Plan	20 years if you're a new borrower on or after July 1, 2014 25 years if you're not a new borrower on or after July 1, 2014

ICR Plan	25 years

Eligible Loan Types

Eligible Loan Type	REPAYE Plan	PAYE Plan	IBR Plan	ICR Plan
Direct Subsidized Loans	Eligible	Eligible	Eligible	Eligible
Direct Unsubsidized Loans	Eligible	Eligible	Eligible	Eligible
Direct PLUS Loans made to Graduate or Professional Students	Eligible	Eligible	Eligible	Eligible
Direct PLUS Loans made to Parents	Not eligible	Not eligible	Not eligible	Eligible if consolidated*
Direct Consolidation Loans that did not Repay any PLUS Loans made to Parents	Eligible	Eligible	Eligible	Eligible

Direct Consolidation Loans that Repaid PLUS Loans made to Parents	Not eligible	Not eligible	Not eligible	Eligible
Subsidized Federal Stafford Loans (from the FFEL Program)	Eligible if consolidated*	Eligible if consolidated*	Eligible	Eligible if consolidated*
Unsubsidized Federal Stafford Loans (from the FFEL Program)	Eligible if consolidated*	Eligible if consolidated*	Eligible	Eligible if consolidated*
FFEL PLUS Loans made to graduate or professional students	Eligible if consolidated*	Eligible if consolidated*	Eligible	Eligible if consolidated*
FFEL PLUS Loans made to parents	Not eligible	Not eligible	Not eligible	Eligible if consolidated*
FFEL Consolidation Loans that did not repay any PLUS loans made to parents	Eligible if consolidated*	Eligible if consolidated*	Eligible	Eligible if consolidated*
FFEL Consolidation	Not eligible	Not eligible	Not eligible	Eligible if

Loans that repaid PLUS loans made to parents				consolidated*
Federal Perkins Loans	Eligible if consolidated*	Eligible if consolidated*	Eligible if consolidated*	Eligible if consolidated*

Student Loan Repayment Checklist:

Pre-Graduate Blueprint:

1. **Review your Federal student loan history**. Get your loan history by going to www.nslds.ed.gov. Review the most important details of your loan:
    - Find out the current loan balance and interest rate for each loan.
    - Find out the type of loan you have (repayment plans depend on when you started school and what loan types you have. Having this information handy will help you to navigate your repayment process).
    - Store the name and contact information of the loan servicer for each loan.
2. **Get to Know your Loan Servicer**. Your loan servicer will help you with your student loans at no charge. Know who they are and how to contact them to ensure that you have direct access to the programs that will make your loan repayment experience as good as possible.
3. **Create an Online Account on your Servicer's Website**. Be proactive by having an online account and an open line of communication with your loan servicer. When you need to start making payments or find the right repayment plan, you'll be ahead of the game.
4. **Complete Mandatory Exit Counseling.** All Federal student loan borrowers must complete exit counseling. Exit counseling educates borrowers on the information and

resources available. It will give a detailed overview of the repayment plans that could work best for you.

Post-Graduate Blueprint:

1. **Know When You Have to Start Making Payments.** For most Federal student loans, you will have six months, or nine months for Federal Perkins Loans after you graduate, leave school, or drop below half-time enrollment before you are required to start making loan payments.
2. **Create a Budget**. Create a budget to determine how much you can afford to pay monthly toward your student loans.
3. **Consider Loan Consolidation**. A Direct Consolidation loan pays off all included loans and starts one new loan with one monthly payment. Loan consolidation allows you to combine loans from multiple servicers, and especially helps with the Federal Family Education Loan (FFEL) Program or Federal Perkins Loans. With a loan consolidation, borrowers can increase their chances of qualifying for an affordable repayment plan and have more loan forgiveness options for the future. Loan consolidation starts the repayment process over. Doing a consolidation soon after the deferment period ends can save borrowers years of interest payments compared to those who wait. This may or may not be the best option if you are already years into a repayment plan.
4. **Set a Goal for Repayment**. S.M.A.R.T. goals for your student loans will help you determine the best repayment plan for yourself. Do you want to pay your loan off as quickly as possible, or do you want the lowest payment that gives you the flexibility to pay it in more time? Once you

know the answer to this question, you can aim for the plan that suits you best.

5. **Select an Affordable Repayment Plan**. With so many repayment plans to choose from, how do you know which is best for you? Work with your loan servicer to discuss your options. With your repayment goals set and a plan in place, you will have a roadmap to paying off your student loan debt.
6. **Know Whether You Are Eligible for Loan Forgiveness Based on Your Employer or Your Job.** Student loan repayment is one of the hottest new employee benefits many companies are offering. Companies like: PriceWaterhouseCoopers, Fidelity, Aetna, and many others are paying thousands of dollars a year towards repayment of student loan debt for employees. Some do it in the form of a contribution to a retirement plan, reimbursements, and direct payments. This makes student loan repayment available to people who don't qualify for traditional loan forgiveness through the Public Service Loan Forgiveness.

Repayment Blueprint:

1. **Make On-Time Payments to Your Loan Servicer**. Your loan servicer will provide you with a loan repayment schedule that tells you when your first payment is due, as well as all other payment details.
2. **Make Repayment Simple. Enroll in Automatic Debit**. Once you enroll, your payments will be automatically taken from your bank account each month. This will help you to stay on track with your payments and as an added bonus, you may get a 0.25% interest rate

deduction if you have Direct Loans. Check your servicer's website for details.

3. **Know Your Options if You Can't Make Your Loan Payment**. If you don't pay the full amount due on time or if you start missing payments, your loan will be considered delinquent and late fees may be charged to you. If you can't make your payments, contact your loan servicer immediately for help. Your servicer can offer you temporary or long-term options, such as changing repayment plans, deferment, forbearance, or loan consolidation.
4. **Reduce Your Federal Income Taxes**. You may be eligible to deduct a portion of the student loan interest you paid on your Federal tax return. Student loan interest payments are reported both to the IRS and to you on IRS Form 1098-E, *Student Loan Interest Statement*. Check with the IRS or a tax advisor to see if you qualify for this deduction.

Student Loan Forgiveness

Imagine a program that forgives your mortgage after ten years or your car loan after two years. It sounds preposterous but that's exactly what Federal student loans do for qualified borrowers. With the various repayment plans offered by loan servicers, there is an opportunity to have the remaining portion of a student loan forgiven.

While most loans are initially scheduled to be paid in ten years, borrowers are given repayment choices that extend the loan repayment time and lower monthly payments. With these options, loan servicers are able to collect more interest over time. For borrowers with financial instability, the low payments allow them to maintain positive credit history while addressing other pressing financial matters in their lives. Some repayment plans allow for payments as low as $0.00/ month.

Unfortunately for these borrowers with low payments or no payment, the interest tab never stops going. Therefore, people who would have expected to pay their loans off in fifteen, or twenty years can see their loans be with them for much longer as a result of their loans capitalizing. This is why loan forgiveness is such a crucial course of action.

So many of my clients talk about their student loans like they're a bad marriage they will never get out of. While bad marriages have divorce, you cannot escape from student loans even if you file bankruptcy. It takes hope away from borrowers and makes them feel like they can't start living their best financial life until they're seventy years old. Making payments for twenty years before loans are forgiven doesn't feel like a shortcut—but it doesn't feel like a life sentence either. When clients see they have twenty years to pay off their loans or they'll be forgiven, seeing the day these loans are paid off is a realistic idea.

Here is a List of all the Student Loan Forgiveness Programs Available:

Public Service Loan Forgiveness (PSLF)

Forgiveness with Income-Based Repayment (IBR)

Forgiveness with Pay As You Earn (PAYE)

Forgiveness with Revised Pay As You Earn (REPAYE)

Forgiveness with Income-Contingent Repayment (ICR)

Federal Perkins Loan Cancellation

Student Loan Forgiveness for Teachers

Student Loan Forgiveness for Nurses

Loan Repayment Assistance for Doctors and Other Health Care Professionals

Loan Repayment Assistance for Lawyers

Military Student Loan Forgiveness and Assistance

Student Loan Discharge for Special Circumstances

Public Service Loan Forgiveness:

Other than loan forgiveness through a repayment plan that takes at least 20 years, the Public Service Loan Forgiveness program is the most popular program. The PSLF program is for people who work in public service jobs with the federal, state, or local government or for a 501C (3) nonprofit organization. Once you are a full-time employee of these qualifying organizations, it doesn't matter if you are the receptionist or groundskeeper, you would be eligible to have 100% of your remaining student loans forgiven after 120 consecutive payments. The program started in 2007, so as of 2017, the first cohort of eligible borrowers would have gotten their loans forgiven. With this process, there are a number of steps that have to be followed initially, and every year, to assure that PSLF works for you.

By following the steps, you can be eligible to have your student loans forgiven. The biggest challenge keeping people from qualifying at this point is being consistent with the yearly updates for income and family size information. It's imperative to complete every step each year to position yourself to be a beneficiary of this program. The negative part of the program is the amount being forgiven may be added as income to your taxes. That can cause you to get less of a tax refund, or leave you with a balance to pay the IRS. Even though this may not be ideal, it can still mean a savings of thousands of dollars and many years of freedom from student loan payments. Little bit by little bit, brick by brick, you will build a path towards paying off your student loans.

Your Blueprint:

- Go to the National Student Loan Data System website (www.nslds.ed.gov) to get all of your up-to-date Federal student loan details.
- Speak with your loan servicer to determine which repayment options are available to you.
- Determine your eligibility for Student Loan forgiveness through repayment plans or forgiveness plans like PSLF.
- See what student loan repayment, reimbursement, or contribution plans your present or future employer offers.

- Submit income and family size information yearly to your loan servicer to maintain eligibility for repayment plans and loan forgiveness.

Chapter SEVEN

The Credit Boosting Blueprint

"Life has no limitations except the ones you set for yourself."

~ Les Brown

Establishing new credit is one of the biggest obstacles for people who have experienced having poor credit or no credit. It's kind of like looking for a job. You can't get the job if you don't have the experience, and you can't get experience unless you get the job. If you don't have a track record of making payments on time, you will be stuck in the same dilemma with your credit. There are a few places you can go to establish conventional credit. Chances are, if you do get approved for a starter line of credit, usually the credit limit will be so low, it could hurt your score just by using that credit line. With such a low limit, once you use it, a high percentage of the utilization will be used, whereby doing more harm than good. Building a strong credit profile can be a challenge; however, it's worth it. If done correctly, you can gain purchasing power for high credit limits and low-interest rates. This is a process, so be willing to take one step at a time. You may not see off the charts progress right away, but in time, you'll have the credit needed to grant you access to real estate, business funding, and much more.

There are many reasons people aren't able to get access to credit. Of course, there are those who are in the midst of a financial struggle and can't get new credit because the credit they have is suffering. This could be because of late payments, collections, foreclosure, or bankruptcy. For those facing these challenges, it's vital you take the time to clear your way out of the fog. Gain clarity on what you can do with your current income to recover from these issues. When you're in a hole, the first thing you need to do is put down the shovel. Getting more credit is hardly the solution when you're struggling with the credit you have.

Another group struggling to get access to credit are those who have had credit challenges in the past and have given up on their credit lives altogether. These are the people for whom bad credit wasn't a series of events, but became apart of who they are. They believe they are bad credit, and act as such. The biggest reason they don't get new credit is they "know" no one will give them credit and they have convinced themselves they don't need credit anyway. This is a dangerous place to be in. The problem is not the fact that this person may have a low score, but that they've attached a mental and emotional label to themselves as a result of their past challenges.

Rich's Story

An example of this is a family friend, Rich. Rich has always been a really hard working guy. He had his own business for years and made good money. At the time, Rich had gone through a divorce six years prior and his credit was ruined. Since that point, he never applied for credit, never thought about buying a house, and paid cash for everything. One day, he saw me recording a video about credit and we started talking about his credit. He told me about his ordeal with credit and how his credit was so bad no one would lend him money for a stick of gum. He eventually let me take a look at this "terrible" credit and to his surprise, just about everything he was worried about had been removed from his credit report. He looked at it and felt like he had a new lease on life. Now highly motivated, he jumped into the credit building process and bought a house within a year. Stories like Rich's are not uncommon. As a matter of fact, they are all too common. People get so stuck to their credit past they never even think of looking at what is on their report so they can repair it. Most bad credit items only have a lifespan of seven years, so, while you may be on the sidelines for a while, your credit is certainly not dead.

People who have never established credit also have a hard time getting started with credit. Without the guidance of where to go to begin, they get faced with denials and apply with the wrong creditors. Having no credit and having bad credit are issues with similar consequences and similar solutions. Starting with secured lines of credit and guaranteed approvals can open the door to building a strong credit profile. This is a nuanced art, yet when used correctly, can save you a year or more on your credit journey. The resources to come have proven successful for many others because they offer a few key elements. They are designed for people with limited or poor credit. They report to the three major credit bureaus and they offer the ability to get higher credit limits either immediately or over time. Study each resource and utilize those that work best for your finances and your life.

Secured Credit Cards

The first thing Rich did when he found out that he had the power to rebuild his credit was to get a secured credit card. These look, act, and report to the credit bureaus just like traditional credit cards, but unlike unsecured credit cards, you have to deposit money into a Certificate of Deposit account of the bank offering the secured line of credit and borrow against those funds. For example, if you got a $500 secured credit card, your credit limit would be secured by a deposit, more than likely, a $500 deposit. This approach is used by many banks to help people establish credit. Most creditors report to the big three bureaus, so each month your credit scores will reflect your payment history. All of the same principles apply when you get a secured credit card. It's important to make your payments on time, keep your balances low, and keep it open, even when you pay off your balance. Secured cards are a great tool to jumpstart credit and get you in the game, or back in the game.

The approval requirements for a secured credit card are significantly less than those for unsecured credit cards. Some banks would approve a borrower for secured credit a day out of bankruptcy, or even if they have no credit history at all. Lending is all about risk and the likelihood a borrower will repay a debt. With someone who has experienced credit hardships, creditors wouldn't want to take the risk unless they got assurances payments would be made. The security of the deposit, equal to the credit line, is that assurance. If you get an unsecured credit card and don't make payments, a creditor can report your delinquencies to the credit bureaus, they can sell your debt to a collection agency, and/or even take legal action to get a judgment.

With secured credit cards, creditors don't run the same risk. If a borrower uses the entire limit and never pays back the borrowed amount, the creditor will close the account and keep the deposit. In addition, they will still pursue you for the past due amount while reporting the delinquencies to the credit bureaus. They still won't make the high amounts of interest they were hoping for, but they don't lose. That's why they give borrowers the opportunity to establish credit using secured credit cards.

While this is a great tool, it runs a few risks borrowers should be aware of. When applying for a secured credit card, ask when the account becomes unsecured and get it in writing. After a year, most creditors would send back the deposit upon request and keep the line of credit open. That way, the gains from a borrower's disciplined payments can be built on. Some creditors close the account once the deposit is returned. Meaning all of the payment history established over the course of a year is closed and limited. There will be a benefit of having a paid-off account showing positive payment history, but when an account is closed, you lose the residual effect of that account's ongoing reporting. Be sure to shop around for the card that is going to work for you now and later. The bank is making money on the money you deposited on top of the interest you're paying every month. By closing the account after the deposit is returned, they're keeping your credit limited so you won't be able to build credit as effectively. You don't want that. Instead, look for a secured credit card willing to return your money after a year and make the credit card unsecured while keeping the account going.

Secured credit cards are a great tool but let's keep going so you can see more powerful options when it comes to building your credit.

Authorized User Accounts

Years ago, I came across a property that was the perfect deal for me. The owner was two years behind on her mortgage and she needed to sell before the bank foreclosed on the house. I had the assets, I had the income, but being twenty years old at the time, I just didn't have the credit. A friend told me if I was added to a credit card, I would be able to get a boost in my credit score. So that's what I did. My grandfather added me to one of his credit cards as an authorized user.

My credit score climbed up over thirty points and I closed on my first property. When you are added as an authorized user to a credit account, also known as piggy-backing, your credit takes on the payment history, balance, and the length of credit of that line of credit. If the cardholder has maintained the card in a positive way, you'll inherit positive results from that account. On the flip side, If they've been late or maxed out, that will also be reflected. Avoid considering doing this with anyone you don't know. If you are not careful, you can lose money and damage your credit doing this. If done correctly, this can save you months or even years on your credit building process.

What is an Authorized User Tradeline?

An authorized user tradeline is one of the most powerful tools in credit. While it's not enough by itself to qualify for a mortgage, it can help boost credit scores significantly. These are lines of credit someone has added you to. Your credit report will reflect the payment history, length of credit, utilization rate, and all factors. If the card is positive in all of those places, it will reflect positively on your credit. The longer a line of credit is open, the more of an impact it will have on your credit. The size of the credit limit is another major factor. With a higher credit limit, the more purchasing power the authorized user will have when applying for their own credit lines. The impact of an authorized user tradeline is one-sided. As long as the person being added to the account is not given access to the credit card by the cardholder, the cardholder is not at risk for having their credit line negatively impacted. Not only that, but if the authorized user has horrible credit, that horrible credit history won't transfer to the cardholder. It's like if you were to give someone money. The receiver's poor money management skills won't be transferred to you. In the same way, a cardholder won't take on bad credit for adding someone as an authorized user.

Who is This For?

Many parents add their children as authorized users to credit cards when they send them off to college. That way their child has access to credit for essentials and emergencies and no, beer is not considered an essential or an emergency.

This can also be used for anyone who has limited credit or poor credit and would like to supplement their credit with a positive tradeline. Piggybacking is a small stepping stone in comparison to the entire path. While your credit score can go up, underwriters for banks and finance companies won't weigh the impact of an authorized user account nearly as much as they do a primary cardholder. If you start your credit building journey with an authorized user tradeline, you'll be approved for higher credit limits and unsecured credit without having to go through the slow process of establishing credit and getting credit limit increases. This process can take a significant amount of time off of the credit building process.

Major Benefit:

Consumers can achieve a quick boost in credit score without incurring any additional debt or credit. This is a great advantage because it's like an E-Z Pass to better credit. For someone starting their credit profile with an authorized user account, they have a great chance of being approved for unsecured credit cards, and in some cases, an auto loan with a decent interest rate.

When Should You Do This?

An authorized user tradeline can show up on a credit profile shortly after the statement date. If someone is planning on making a major purchase, they should do this at least a month before applying for credit to get the benefits of the account. For someone looking to buy a house, this should be done at the beginning of the credit building process. If the future home buyer has limited credit, they could get an authorized user tradeline thirteen months before applying for a home, then apply for two unsecured credit cards over $1,000, and once those accounts are a year old, their credit would be strong enough to qualify for a mortgage with the help of minor credit supplements. It will help you attain lines of credit with higher limits than if you didn't have that line of credit at all. If you are renting a tradeline or an authorized user account, you would want to start the process at least thirty days before you go for any of your credit approvals.

Easy Credit Approval Accounts

The companies shared in this section are resources with opportunities to build credit when other companies may deny you. What makes these companies useful is they give higher credit limits than conventional methods of credit building. Keep in mind that companies do come and go, therefore, do your due diligence before you use any of them.

These have been some of the primary tools my business uses to help people obtain funding and generally build stronger credit. Each one has a quality making it particularly unique and effective. If you are suffering from limited credit, these can help solve the issue of getting approved for credit. With positive payment history on these items, it could open you up to higher credit limits with top tier credit vendors. Higher credit limits, positive payment history, and low utilization with top tier credit vendors will lead to you proving creditworthiness. Study each of these thoroughly to determine if they can assist you in creating and building your own blueprint.

Out of the available options, I recommend starting with the one you feel the most comfortable with. Depending on the severity of your credit and the number of lines you have or need, choose others to supplement your profile as well. Be patient and diligent. As easily as these items can help to build your credit, they can also hurt your credit if you overdo it and take on more than you can manage.

My Jewelers Club

This tool has had a few issues recently but what it has done for many of my clients is given them a $5,000 line of credit when jewelry is purchased from their website. It offers easy credit approvals. The size of the credit line really helps with the credit building process because, after a purchase, you will have a small balance in relation to the $5,000 credit limit you possess. This will give you a very low utilization rate for this tradeline.

They charge a $100 membership fee but outside of bankruptcy, tax liens, and severe negligence you will be able to qualify for a $5,000 line of credit. Even with some of those credit issues, you may still be approved. The significance of the size of the credit line is that mortgage banks and other creditors look at how much credit you're capable of managing. To qualify for a home loan, having three or more lines of credit with limits over $1,000 will help you meet the basic criteria. When you consider traditional banks would offer $300-$500 accounts to limited credit borrowers, high lines of credit will expedite the building process significantly faster.

What is My Jewelers Club?

My Jewelers Club is an online jewelry company, offering financing with easy credit approvals. Now, please understand, the jewelry is by far not the best part of this service, however, the best of what they do offer is a means to an end.

Taking advantage of this service can help you add twenty-fifty points to your credit report within one credit reporting cycle. If you are looking for a quick boost on your credit score, this could be for you.

My recommendation is to secure this line of credit at least sixty days before applying for any meaningful credit, such as a mortgage. The longer you are able to keep the account before making an application, the better.

For more information and to get started, visit their website: http://bit.ly/creditgems.

RENTAL KHARMA

What is Rental Kharma?

For anyone renting, Rental Kharma allows you to add your rental history to your credit report, with a fee of course. Rent is one of the largest bills consumers pay, and up until now, it only impacted your credit if you had a negative history. With this service, you will be able to retrospectively add your positive rental payments from as far back as two years to your credit report. This can have a major impact on your length of credit. For those who have new credit, this would help you establish two years of credit history in as little as fifteen business days. There are other rental history reporting companies popping up as well, therefore, do your research before signing up for any of them. There are some management companies who offer credit reporting capabilities. To that end, check with them first.

There is however one drawback. Rental Kharma only reports to your Transunion credit report and only that bureau will reflect the added length of credit and payment history.

Nevertheless, despite it only reporting to one bureau, in my opinion, it's still worthwhile to have it as a tradeline. Once it's there, it can't be ignored.

For more information and to get started, visit their website: Rentalkharma.com.

Self Lender

Self Lender is an innovative spin on a traditional way to start building credit. With no credit score needed, it's simply a savings account that reports as a loan on your credit report. Borrowers make a payment each month, which is essentially a deposit every month. What makes it different and a powerful credit resource is that each deposit is reported to the credit bureaus like a payment. This allows you to build credit while saving money. It is similar to a secured credit card, but the major difference is you don't have to deposit a large sum of money up front to get started.

Along with administrative fees to get started, you simply deposit dollar amounts as low as $49/month, which is put into an interest-bearing account that simultaneously generates a positive payment history as you go. At the moment, this line of credit is available nationwide, except in New York, Wisconsin, and Vermont. For those eligible, Self Lender helps with two major criteria in the mortgage approval process. It helps to build credit and the savings aspect of it helps with the assets required to qualify. The funds are held in a Certificate of Deposit (CD) until maturity.

Self Lender will have the maximum impact if you start building this account a year in advance of getting approved for your mortgage. The ongoing theme here is to start this process as soon as possible and as early in advance of buying your home as possible. The sooner you establish your Self Lender account, the better.

With Self Lender, you will be able to establish a line of credit of $1,100. To qualify for a mortgage, you must establish at least three tradelines, open for a year or more with a credit limit of $1,000. Also, you get to save money and accrue interest on the money you are saving. The fees are low and the results are huge.

For more information and to get started, visit their website: https://www.selflender.com.

Earlier I mentioned how Rich was surprised that his credit was not as bad as he thought it was. He took that information and made himself a homeowner within a year. This is what we did to make homeownership possible for someone who just a short time before, thought his credit was hopeless.

Rich's Blueprint:

- Rich got a copy of his credit report. There are many options to choose from. This step was the most important step because you cannot achieve success if you do not believe you can do it. His report showed him that it was possible.
- He got a secured credit card. My preferred option is Self Lender rather than a secured credit card, but Self Lender does not operate in New York and a few other states as of now. Rich had cash, so he was able to get a $1,000 secured credit card to reestablish his credit.
- He got approved for a $5,000 line of credit with My Jewelers Club. He was not the jeweler type of guy, but the impact it would have on his credit made it worthwhile for him to get an inexpensive watch.
- Right before he started the Pre-Approval process to buy the house he was renting, he added Rental Kharma. Since they report rent retroactively, Rich only needed to add this at the end of the credit building process to have the required number of credit accounts to get approved for a favorable mortgage loan.

Chapter EIGHT

The Blueprints – Pulling It All Together

The blueprint for success is inside you. It will stay there unless you take it out and create it.

~ Larina Kase

Building excellent credit is a process that can be like putting together a puzzle. It is a combination of the right moves at the right time where, in time, it shows a beautiful picture. We now have all the pieces on the table. Whether it was understanding credit to buy a house, getting funding for your business, or just because you liked the cover, reading to this point has given you incredible insight on everything credit is and does. At this phase, we must answer one question, "How do I make this work for me?"

I'm glad you asked. People who are just starting out with credit and those who are overcoming credit challenges face completely different journeys. The examples to follow will show the steps each type of consumer can follow to take all of this information and put it to use.

New Credit Profile

Most people don't learn about credit until they mess it up. If you are fortunate enough to start building credit with the guidance of this book, you will be miles ahead of others, like me, who had to take the more testing path. A new credit profile is like fertile soil that'll reap what is sown. If there are positive credit habits planted, with consistency and time, there will be low-interest credit offered and opportunities to harvest. If there is neglect, overuse, and inconsistency, then you'll sow denial of credit and debt.

Jackie's Story

Jackie came to me well into her thirties. Her mother taught her credit was bad and that "if you can't buy it cash, then you can't afford it." She held onto those words and never took out a dollar of credit to buy anything. She paid her way through college, her cars had always been paid for in cash, and she owed nothing to anyone. Only Jackie had been renting for the last fourteen years and her landlord wanted to sell his house to her. Though she had saved up quite a bit of money, Jackie didn't have the money to pay for the house in cash. In essence, she couldn't afford it! At least according to the way she'd been taught. Still, she knew this was an opportunity she wasn't willing to pass up without a fight.

She went to a mortgage banker and was told to get a secured credit card and come back in a year. The house wasn't going to be available to buy in a year. She'd be renting from a new owner in a year if this was the final answer. She called me with anxiety and fear because to her, I was her last hope. When we did a quick review of her credit report and it was quick because there was nothing there, there were no credit cards, student loans, collection accounts, nothing. Other than her name and personal information, her credit report was blank. This is truly a rare occurrence for a person in their thirties, but for us, it was a great opportunity to build the perfect credit profile.

While no credit is looked at as bad credit, a blank report is easy to build, if done correctly. For someone in Jackie's position with no credit and a small window to access credit, I recommended the following.

Jackie's Blueprint:

1. Create a budget. No matter what you are doing, credit or finance related, start with a budget! The budget will help to clarify what money you can assign to an expense, savings, and your goals. In Jackie's case, we wanted to get clear on what she could afford to pay for a mortgage and how aggressively she could build her credit profile.
2. Jackie established a Self Lender account (*Do your own due diligence before signing up*). Self Lender does what a secured credit card does only better. Jackie got the $1,000 line of credit because $1,000 is the magic number for credit limits when getting a mortgage.
3. Next, Jackie applied for a My Jewelers Club account (*Do your own due diligence before signing up*). They give a $5,000 line of credit to all their "Members" who sign up for an account. Also, they require a purchase to be made to get the line of credit. Jackie was left with a balance of $100 making her utilization rate for this line of credit 2%, which

is very low and helped to drive her credit score up. Again, considering this is a brand new line of credit for her, it still didn't solve the length of credit portion of the equation but it strengthened the utilization rate and offered a high credit limit that would be viewed favorably to underwriters.

4. Then, she signed up for Rental Kharma. While this only reports to Transunion, it hits the credit report and that's all an underwriter needs to see. It's not a major factor in increasing a credit score but it does what no other line of credit does. It reports retroactively. It allows you to add the last two years of rental history to your credit report for a fee. In Jackie's case, the fee was well worth it because it was an investment getting her closer to home ownership. The other lines of credit helped her to reach the credit line limit requirement from the lender and that helped to boost the score. Rental Kharma played a unique role since now she had two years of credit history when there was none before.
5. Make payments on new credit lines. For Jackie, we needed her to get the seller to agree to sell in six months. In doing so, the time frame provided her with the room needed for her score to increase well above the 700 range. The limited credit was still an obstacle but her credit profile was a lot stronger since now she had three lines of credit. With the help of alternative credit (rent, cable bill, gym membership, utility bill, etc) that her mortgage banker allowed her to use her credit was strong enough to close on her own home in just seven months. This may not be the case for everyone, but this process was life-changing for Jackie.
6. (Optional) For those looking to get financing for a vehicle or needing a boost in their credit score, have a family member or friend add them as an authorized user. With a responsible cardholder who pays on time and maintains

low credit balances, a consumer can benefit from inheriting positive credit history and improve the credit score and length of credit history. This would not be sufficient as a stand-alone strategy but in concert with other credit building vehicles, it can be a great supplement for obtaining credit.

7. With a new and growing credit profile, you will be open to a whole new world of financing just like Jackie. With these lines of credit in place, you will have a tremendous starting position for excellent credit in a short period of time. Now, you can apply for a top tier credit card. By applying for a national bank credit card, you cement your credit profile and give it a platform to grow further. The purpose is not to get more debt but to have access to more credit, and that's what this process will do.

Jackie's case was unique because she never established credit. With a blank slate, the credit building process can be easy in comparison to someone who has bumps, bruises, or even crashes on their credit. If everyone was like Jackie, my job would be easy. However, they're not. Most people are more like Paul. Paul made me work to make him a success story. In all reality, Paul couldn't have gotten over his credit challenges if he wasn't willing to work for it. He wanted it and he earned his success.

Paul's Story

Paul owned a sports apparel company. He's been grinding hard for his big break. Year after year, he would bid on big contracts to provide schools in New York City with gear for gym class and their sports teams. However, he failed year after year. There's one thing you should know about Paul. He'd been told he couldn't do "it" his whole life. When he heard no or met failure, he went back to the drawing board and came back better. After years of relentlessly pursuing a big contract, he had the winning bid! Can you imagine the exhilaration, the joy, and the relief that he finally did it? The big "OH YES" quickly turned into a big "OH SHOOT" when he realized he had to fulfill huge orders he never had the pressure of handling before. These big apparel companies had the capital and credit to wait to get paid or use lines of credit to get the gear manufactured. Paul didn't have the capital and he definitely didn't have the credit.

I answered the phone and on the other end was a frantic business owner who was afraid of losing everything he'd been working for. Paul explained to me if he couldn't fulfill this order, he could be blacklisted with the Board of Education in New York and never get a contract with them again. He began to wish he'd stuck to the small jobs he had been getting from them. He could do that in his sleep, but this was a different story. He couldn't get a credit line because he had delinquent student loans he hadn't paid attention to for six years. He had medical bills piled up from when he'd gotten sick. All he had positive was a small credit card he'd had for two years that was unfortunately always maxed out and a car loan, which was almost repossessed two years prior.

One major thing to keep in mind is that recent events have the biggest impact on your credit. If you had a late payment last month, it will have a more severe impact than a late payment from two years ago. Credit wounds heal with time just like real wounds. In Paul's case, he had little positive transactions to counteract the negative history with. Time was of the essence. It was January and he needed to produce his wares by August.

Paul's Blueprint:

1. Not budgeting had left Paul playing Russian Roulette with his finances and his business. He would often overdraft his account because money was constantly going in and out and he didn't sweat the negative dollars in his account because he knew more money was coming. My thought was to immediately get him on a budget. I explained this was a matter of life or death...to his business. If he didn't learn how to budget now, he could run his business into bankruptcy. When he got bigger contracts and responsibilities, he could also get blacklisted in his business community for not being able to deliver his service, because he didn't have cash on hand. He was serious about taking his business and life to the next level, so he committed to budgeting.

2. Paul had fallen off the wagon with his student loan payments. He felt like he was at a point of hopelessness. He didn't think he would ever be able to get back on track with them. Consumer debt may fall off of credit reports after seven years and ten for bankruptcy but student loans have to be paid! I told him to call his loan servicer, get into the Loan Rehabilitation program, and within nine months all of his late payment history would be brought current. This is the only debt that does this. He got into the Loan Rehabilitation Program, got on a payment plan, and something miraculous happened. In only five months, the student loan servicer reported six years of non-payments as

payments made on time. This is when he started feeling like this was really going to work.

3. Dispute inaccurate or unverifiable items on your credit report using the Fair Credit Reporting Act. We sent dispute letters to each of the "Big 3" credit bureaus, challenging the areas of the debt we knew had inaccuracies. In Paul's case, he had gotten collection letters and calls about medical bills and other debt. The first round of the dispute campaign came back with six items deleted and three verified. We were not satisfied with the results of the disputes so we took our disputes to the next level. They were eventually removed from his credit.

4. Paul continued making existing payments on time. He had a high-interest car note he hated paying every month. He was being ripped off but he continued to make the payments until he could sell the car once he got the funding he needed. The larger the debt, the bigger the impact it has on your credit report. By making his car loan payments on time, he organically improved his credit. This essentially was the foundation his credit was being built on. He had the loan for a few years. Although he missed consecutive payments years ago, the recent payment history was positive, and it was the primary reason he had a shot at getting funding. He also had a small credit card that was now being paid on time. As these payments were made, there was a gradual increase in the credit score. They were establishing a new story. With the student loan late payments being reversed, and the collection accounts being removed, Paul saw his credit reach into the 600s for the first time in years.

5. Paul was added to two authorized user tradelines. His mother was willing to help him however she could. When she learned she would not be impacted by her son's credit history, she was happy to be able to help Paul. We'd been working hard to make improvements to Paul's credit. Yet, he was still lacking the number of lines of credit an underwriter was going to look for. Also, his length of credit was weak. Where he was weak, his mother's tradelines were strong. They had been open for over ten years, had high credit limits, low balances, and were never late. This pulled his score over the top and put him in the low 700s. What looked like a hopeless case, suddenly looked like a sure thing. We were almost there.

6. Paul got a credit limit increase on the small limit credit card he had. Before he called to get a credit limit increase, he paid down the balance on the card, kept it low, and made early payments every month from the time we started the process. By the time the student loan was rehabilitated and the medical collections were removed, he demonstrated he was a more responsible borrower. With the authorized user accounts boosting his score, he was able to get a credit limit increase. The reason the credit limit increase was important is not that he wanted to charge more on his credit card but because having a higher limit on his accounts would justify other lenders giving him larger lines of credit and improve his utilization ratio.
7. Paul's credit had come full circle. He went from having late payments all over his credit report, to having been repaired and rehabilitated. His results aren't uncommon. The reason the repair happened so fast was because he was on top of every element of the process, and he hired great help.

Being that his business had been generating revenue for years, his new and improved credit helped him to get the funding he needed. He was able to change his business and his life. He is a testament to what can happen when you believe and never give up. He now has added schools throughout New York and New Jersey to his list of clients. His company is growing rapidly and his credit is now an asset and not a liability. His process was a combination of good principles and aggressive implementation. Each case is going to be unique in some way or another.

The key is to build a solid foundation on budgeting and good money management. Many people get their credit repaired only to be in the same credit dilemma in a few years or even months. Until the core issues are addressed, credit repair is at best, putting lipstick on a pig. Paul is a believer. He knows he can keep his finances on track by spending the time to monitor his income and expenses and to be intentional about where his money goes. Anyone can do the same. Believe me, if Paul could do it, you can do it. He was haphazard with his money and too busy to budget until he faced a make or break situation. The other elements would have only worked temporarily if the deeper work was not done.

When someone undergoes a credit transformation, the outcome is beautiful. It doesn't only affect the credit score. Like Paul, people who "get it" take on a new persona. They interact with their financial decisions in a conscious and intentional way. All too often, people let their credit suffer because they are caught up in the hustle of life and juggle responsibilities with the best intentions. Life never stops coming at you. So when that one thing takes you a step beyond your capacity to keep up, one thing or everything comes crashing down. Those who have decided to be empowered while dealing with their finances are buoyed by systems. A budget, a debt payment plan, payment automation, are those systems that make this process an inevitable success. With this level of control over credit and finances, one can set their sights on bigger targets and know that they can manage it.

Now that you're at a point where your goals are within reach, the question is, what would it take to get to higher level goals? What's next? Let's assume you got your house with a low-interest mortgage payment. You got a car loan at a low-interest rate, and it's almost paid off. Let's say you have a business that sustains itself, but you're ready to take it to the next level and scale up. Good credit can get you a car or a house but you need higher level credit to get a high limit credit line. The difference can be made when you enhance the finer details in your credit. There's one set of rules to get you on the right path, but there's another to get you to the peak, where credit is concerned.

Credit Optimization

As in anything in life, the better you pay attention to details, the better the results. When it comes to credit, it is seldom a zero-sum game. Therefore, you can reach many of your credit goals just by following the basic principles of good credit. Walking every day can keep you healthy, but running every day will keep you fit. That's the difference between taking the steps to optimize your credit and not. We're going into the weeds to give you strategies and areas of focus to position yourself to get your credit into the higher echelons. Credit scores go as high as 850. Most people never reach those heights because even if they generally have good credit, they lack the insight to get the most out of their credit.

Here, we are going to work through every area of the credit report to take points from anywhere we can. The way you can ensure you get the best results is by making sure your credit report is accurate and doesn't have unnecessary information that doesn't help you. The first step is to audit your credit report from top to bottom. Compared to analyzing your credit to prepare for credit disputes, this audit is going to look more deeply into each line of credit to determine if you are achieving the maximum impact from each item. It's less focused on what's being reported and more on the efficiency of the line itself. The details we will be looking at will be based on taking what you learned previously about the five credit factors to a higher degree.

Payment History

Payment history has the greatest impact on a credit score. If taking your credit score from a 720 to the 800s matters to you, making payments on time isn't your challenge. However, you can make it seamless so you can concentrate on improving the other areas of focus. The key to assuring payment history remains a strength is automation. How you do it is what will make the difference for someone who has good credit and aspires for excellent credit.

Making It Automatic

Under conventional wisdom, automating all of your credit bills will make sure you don't forget about making a payment. This is great advice and has proven to be effective. This is done by calling each creditor and having the minimum payment or the amount you choose to be automatically withdrawn from your bank account. It's always important to do this in conjunction with budgeting, to ensure you are accounting for the money in your account so you don't fall short of the payment and end up with a late payment. Once you set it, you can forget it, and spend your mental energy elsewhere.

While this is great, it actually gets better.

Synchronizing Payments and Reporting:

A key element in setting up automatic payments is making sure money will be in the account at the time that the payment is being withdrawn. Once that's established, you can consider getting the most out of this process. Each creditor has a due date that usually coincides with when the account was established. Because of that, you can have a payment due on the 3rd of the month for one bill, the 10th for another, and the 27th for the other. Automation takes the stress of having to go through the process of manually keeping track of and making payments on each account that you owe. What it doesn't do is give you the power to make payments when it works best for your finances. Due dates aren't set in stone. You have the flexibility with almost all the debt to choose the payment date to a time of the month that works best for you. If you get paid on the 1st, it probably won't be convenient for you to have to make a payment on the 30th. If you get paid weekly, it may not be convenient for you to have all of your due dates on the 1st of the month. The placement of a due date on the calendar can be as much of a problem for people living from paycheck to paycheck as their ability to manage money. If you take that challenge away, life can become easier for almost anybody. If you had it your way, what day of the month would you pay your bills? Sorry, the answer cannot be "no day" until you're debt-free! Since you know what day that is now, change it!

Step 1:

Review your income for the last three months. Write down the days and weeks of the month you get your income.

Step 2:

Determine what time of the month you have the most money in your account.

Step 3:

Review your credit statements. Write out the dates each bill is due.

Step 4:

Call each creditor to schedule payments to be automatically made based on your income and financial best interest. You can have all your bills automatically withdrawn on a particular day if that works for you or you can spread them out weekly. Do what works best for you, but try to limit the number of days payments are being made.

Step 5:

Review bank statements at least weekly. If there is an issue like an account being hacked or overdrawn, you'll want to fix it before you start to get late payments.

Synchronizing Your Reporting Date

Now that your payments are automated in the most powerful way, you can look to get the maximum benefit for what can be consistent and automatic credit growth. Creditors report the payments you made or didn't make to the credit bureaus once a month. Each creditor and credit item can have a different reporting date, just like they can have different due dates. They do not automatically position the reporting dates to accommodate consumers. Like due dates, these reporting dates can be changed to suit you.

Why does this even matter? I'm glad you asked! Many people use credit for an automated bill or run up the balance and pay it off by the end of the month. If your balance is at the highest point for when it is reported to the credit bureaus, it will reflect your credit in the least favorable light. You would want to be judged at the end of a diet when you are at an optimal weight rather than at the beginning, right? The point is, you can choose the time when your credit is judged by the credit bureaus every month, and the way to do that is to adjust the date your credit is reported by each creditor. The impact it will have may not be drastic like removing negative items from a credit report. It will be a source of consistent and steady growth as your credit balances will be reported at their lowest amounts for the month, every month.

For Example:

Card Limit: $1,000

Usage for a Month: $500

Payment: $300

Ending Balance: $200

Utilization Rate= Balance / Credit limit (as a percentage)

Utilization at high balance point: ($500/ $1,000) 50%

Utilization at lowest balance point: ($200/ $1,000) 20%

As you can see, when you're intentional about when you make your payments and structure your payments to be made to suit you, you can keep your utilization rate lower on each debt each month. This won't be worth 40 or 50 credit points, but these are points most people are leaving on the table right now. This is the next level of automating your credit so your credit success is on cruise control and your GPS is set to your maximum credit score.

Optimizing Utilization When Buying a Car

According to Finder.com, 44% of adults rely on auto financing to get a car. Almost all of those people buy without a strategic plan to build credit while doing it. When my friend Rob needed to buy a car, I showed him this technique that really paid dividends for him. Most people have a budget on how much they are willing to put down on a car. Rob had good credit and $7,000 to put down on a new car listed for $30,000. That's a reasonable amount to put down for such a sizable purchase. I told him to put that amount down—but he shouldn't do it like everyone else.

Instead, I told him to do this:

- Determine how much you want to put down on the car purchase.
- Get a loan for little or no money down.
- On the 1st payment, pay the predetermined amount that you intended to put down.
- His credit limit reflected on the credit report would be $30,000.
- His balance after one month would be $23,000.

When you put money down on a loan, it is not reflected in the credit limit or balance on your credit report. If the loan after the down payment is $10,000, then the credit limit is $10,000 and the balance is $10,000. That's a 100% utilization. While you are not penalized for utilization as harshly with installments as you are with revolving debt, it still will be a negative on your credit. By getting the loan with 0% down and applying your intended down payment to the remaining balance, you start your loan with a lower utilization percentage and start your loan off with a much better credit position than if you paid the down payment before the loan as most people do. Now you get to maximize the credit benefit while using the same amount of money.

Ideal Credit Mix

Credit mix represents a small percentage of what a credit file is built on. The small details do matter though. Credit should always be pursued for a specific goal. I don't recommend getting credit you may not need just for the sake of getting credit or building the perfect credit score. The only exception is when someone is buying a house and has not established the requisite credit lines up to that point. Having the ideal credit mix should be the function of organic credit building. With that said, this is the breakdown of what a very strong credit file looks like:

- Revolving Credit/ Credit Cards: 3-6
- High Limits ($10,000+)
- Low Balances
- From National Banks
- Opened for More Than Four Years

- Installments (*Credit to be paid off in a defined period of time*): 2-4
- Includes Car loans, Furniture, Personal loans, Student loans, etc.
- Best credit score benefit after paying off 70% of each loan

----

- Mortgages: 1-2

With this type of a credit profile, the maximum credit score is achievable. The credit mix is still such a small part of the equation, everything else has to be perfect. As long as you've accounted for the other credit factors, this credit mix will take you to the highest levels of credit.

Levels of credit:

All credit cards are not created equal. There are companies that will extend credit to people who have poor credit and there are lenders that will only lend to consumers with excellent credit. Cards that are easier to qualify for tend to be lower tier creditors. These are generally smaller companies who are taking the chance with risky consumers because they can make big margins on their product if a certain percentage of their customers repay their debt. Higher tier creditors have strict lending measures because they are beholden to larger investors and stockholders. They generally offer lower interest rates, and while they make tons of money, they take a more conservative approach to lending. Based on how well established these creditors are with the credit bureaus, their credit holds different weight to a credit report.

Here is a breakdown of how credit cards are weighed:

1. Mall Credit Card: (*40% of maximum reporting value*)

These are the small stores that offer you credit to buy their product. This credit can't be used outside of their brand. They are usually offering credit from a small financial company.

2. Department Store Credit Cards: (*60% of maximum reporting value*)

Malls are anchored by large department stores. In most malls in most cities, you can find the same set of players who the mall is built around. Macy's, Home Depot, Nordstrom, and J.C. Penney are some of the traditional flagship stores that fit this bill. They are big enough to provide their own financing but too limited with their credit offerings to be on a higher credit scale.

3. National Credit Card Companies (*80% of maximum reporting value*)

American Express, Discover, and Capital One are the primary lenders in this range. They are national powers in the credit card world but fall short of the strength of national banks.

4. National Bank Credit Card: (*100% of maximum reporting value*)

Chase, Bank of America, Wells Fargo and other national banks allow you to get the most out of your credit. Consumers have to build up their credit before they'd be eligible for unsecured credit, but once they have established credit, these creditors will reflect most powerfully on credit.

Your Blueprint:

- Review your credit report for any inaccuracies.
- Determine what you need funding for.

- Add one or more of these credit building accounts to your credit to boost your credit profile.
- Add a high limit, low balance authorized user account to your credit.
- Automate payments and synchronize credit due dates, reporting dates to meet your income schedule.

Once you make the decision to get started, you too can create a blueprint to take you all the way. The past is the past. The future is waiting for you. If you make the most out of your present, you will get most of what you want and more. This book can be the step-by-step guide that walks you through your past challenges and takes you to a new reality. Credit is only scary or complicated because you did not have this in your hands before. Now you do. Have faith in who you are and what you can do. I'm certain you've accomplished far greater things in life aside from attaining a 700 credit score before. Therefore, I'm also certain, excellent credit is now within your reach. If homeownership matters to you, if getting better credit health matters to you, if having access to credit matters to you, go get it. You have all the information you need. Now go apply it and watch the transformation happen in your life.

I'd love for you to stay connected with me. I'd be honored to hear about your credit journey and how this book, my courses, and trainings have helped you in any way. You are a success story waiting to happen and I can't wait to celebrate you!

NOTES FROM THE AUTHOR

If you're reading this page, this means, I owe you a congratulations and a huge thank you! Congratulations for having made it through the entire blueprint to building excellent credit and thank you for allowing my words to resonate with you. For those who've read up through this point, I wrote this book for you and I couldn't be happier!

I would like to ask, while this book has gone through an innumerable amount of edits, should you find something we didn't catch, feel free to email me with the correction at coach@yourcreditcoach.com. In addition, to share your stories of improved credit from the products and programs of Your Credit Coach, please email them to me at coach@yourcreditcoach.com as well.

After reading this, if you feel this book has helped you in any way, it would mean so much if you provided an honest online review through Amazon as well as on social media, using the following hashtag, **#yourcreditcoach**. I would equally love it if you believe this book would be of assistance to your friends, family, and your community if you referred them our way.

Thanks again for sticking with me this far, now let's go and build excellent credit!

Contact Us to Learn More About Our:

- Credit Building Services
- Do It Yourself Credit Course
- Home Buying Course

Book Your Credit Coach, LLC for:

- Youth Financial Literacy Workshops
- Credit Building Workshops
- Home Buying Workshops

Contact Your Credit Coach, LLC:

(888) 869-0422

coach@yourcreditcoach.com

Follow us:

@yourcreditcoach

#yourcreditcoach

www.yourcreditcoach.com